ALL THE PAINTINGS OF
GIORGIONE

VOLUME THREE
in the
Complete Library of World Art

The Complete Library of World Art

ALL THE PAINTINGS

OF GIORGIONE, *Giorgio Barbarelli*

Text by LUIGI COLETTI

Translated by PAUL COLACICCHI

OLDBOURNE

London

© 1961 by Rizzoli Editore, Milan
Published in Great Britain by
Oldbourne Press, 121 Fleet Street,
London E.C.4

*Printed in Great Britain by
Jarrold and Sons Ltd, Norwich*

CONTENTS

GIORGIONE

Life and Work

VERY little is known definitely about Giorgione. It is certain that he died young, at the age of thirty-three or thirty-four, in Venice during the plague in the autumn of 1510; that he had gone to Venice from the countryside near Treviso, more precisely from Castelfranco in the immediate neighborhood; that in 1507–8 he received many important commissions; that after his death the most sophisticated collectors were competing for his works, while other painters were busily turning out imitations of his pictures. For this reason, there was a sudden confusion in attributions between Giorgione's paintings and those by other contemporary artists, especially Titian.

Upon these few known facts the legend was built: that he was born into the noble family of Barbarella (which is possible but not proved); that he was jealous of other painters and particularly of Titian; that he loved music, and had many love affairs.

Forty years after his death Vasari wrote a profile of the master, placing him in a perspective which made later Venetian critics conclude that not only was there a parallel to be drawn between Giorgione and Leonardo da Vinci, but that the former had very much the same influence upon modern painting, as we understand it today, in the Veneto, as Leonardo had on Tuscan painting.

Giorgione's "Leonardismo" was not accepted by Boschini or Lanzi; but a recent school of thought, headed by Hourticq and Suida, and rejected by L. Venturi and Fiocco, would replace Giorgione by Titian as the reformer of Venetian art, and would present Giorgione on the exclusive basis of the information given by M. A. Michiel, who was almost a contemporary of his. The author feels, however, that Michiel's facts do not invalidate Vasari's presentation.

Giorgione's language and poetry, his *ratio videndi* and *ratio pingendi*, which we shall strive to define from the group of paintings definitely attributed to him, can be based upon three pictures universally recognized as his work: *The Castelfranco Madonna* (plates 42–46), *The Three Philosophers* (plates 48–53) and the *Gypsy and Soldier* (plates 54–60). In fact, the *Gypsy and Soldier* would suffice, since there can be no doubt about its authorship. We may even dispense from using as a term of reference the *Sleeping Venus* (plates 68–71), which the author ascribes to Giorgione, although others do not.

Binocular vision has by now become such a part of our experience that we no longer realize its admirable complexity, which appears to grip reality in a vice. It is due to the super-imposition and the blending of two similar impressions that we can see an object concretely, in all its relief.

Contrarily, as the object moves away from us the angle of vision become narrower, until it vanishes—theoretically *ad infinitum*, but practically long before that—when the rays, having become parallel, no longer produce a three dimensional effect since the two images can no longer blend. At that point all sense of relief will disappear.

Similarly, for those who use only one eye, the shadows

upon a hillside do not help to define every detail of the surface in relation to the source of light, so that, while they may see the volume of the hillside against the plain, it will appear completely flat. In other words, it will no longer have a plastic function, but merely a chromatic one. An image, therefore, as it moves away from the eye, will lose in weight, in thickness and in detail, but at the same time it will gain in lightness, in transparency and in universality. What vision loses in tactile potentiality, it gains in chromatic possibilities in an equal measure. All these facts had been partially noticed and recorded by Leonardo da Vinci, but other artists had also understood them, and had even translated them into pictorial terms. Let us mention Michelangelo, for instance, and consider the small nude figures in the background of the Doni tondo. They are the result of a few quick transparent touches of the brush; their plastic value is extremely limited if compared with the very elaborate modeling of the foreground group. They prove that the painter was essentially a sculptor, and therefore dominated by plastic interests. He could see and represent distant figures as pure color, devoid of all plasticity. For him, the only function of that particular background was to stress the effect of relief and increase the solidity of the figures in the foreground.

The secret of Giorgione was merely that he saw the whole spectacle of the world as a non-tangible but exclusively visible distance. He reduced the whole of his representation to "pure color". This is the moment when painting becomes really and only painting, giving up all claims to emulate or simulate sculpture or, worse still, to offer an equivalent rather than an image of reality. From this moment the Renaissance's ambiguous and illusive formula of the imitation of nature was superseded. For Renaissance artists color and movement had, of course, some value—let us recall Vasari's insistence upon the merits of painting the "breath of life and warmth of human flesh"—but their main preoccupation was still with third dimensional representation.

Vasari, however, acknowledged the novelty of Giorgione's position on the technical side when he recorded that Giorgione used to paint directly with color, without first drawing the entire composition on the panel, as he was convinced that this was "the real and indeed the best way of drawing". Naturally, Vasari deplored this method, and even saw in it the root of all the evils which he imputed to the Venetian painters.

Obviously there were points of contact, reciprocal influences and limited coincidences between the Florentine and the Venetian schools. I think, however, that one should stress the fundamental and traditional distinction between the mainly plastic interest of the former and the pictorial eminence of the latter.

There was, in fact, a radical difference in the two methods of creating images. While the Florentines, on the one hand, based their representation upon volumetric assessment and considered color merely as an accessory, the Venetians began by conceiving an initial chromatic impression to which they then added muscle and bone. The former used chiaroscuro as a starting point, the latter color. These two methods have been described by Cennini in Chapter 67 of his *Trattato*: here the first one is called "the good method" and the second one "the method used by those who know little about art".

For the Venetians, therefore, all graphic preparation such as drawing, which for the Tuscans was the essential foundation of the image, was reduced to the function of a mnemonic aid, a sort of topographical note for the coagulation of color. This, as related to Giorgione's circle, can be seen in the attributed panel, *The Finding of Romulus and Remus*, now in Frankfurt (plate 101). The graphic points of support, or landmarks, upon which the pictorial structure was to rest, are still visible, and it does not matter whether this was due to the painting being unfinished or to the erosion of time.

Da Vinci himself recommended that the use of preparatory sketches did not require the elements to be carefully finished. This, however, was not an encouragement to imprecision. Leonardo's sketches were often abbreviated and *sous-entendu*, but never evasive; indeed, as is clearly visible in some of his works which never went beyond the preparatory stage, they were always in the nature of a commitment. The *Circumscription*, the "respect for the boundary" imposed by Alberti is still ever present in Da Vinci's work as a precise suggestion of form.

After all, the two different and even contrasting directions taken by the Florentine and Venetian schools can be derived from the ancient distinction seen by Lysippus between representing men, objects and the world as one sees them and as they are, between appearance and essence and between contingency and substance. In other words, while, by the usual Florentine procedure, the image is born, lives and concludes itself in the imagination, though still under the constant control of the intellect, the Venetian's imagination seems rather to play upon the senses. This does not mean that the latter is tantamount to automatism, but rather that the Venetian's research moves away from a mathematical consideration of reality's volumetric structure, toward the immediate assumption of reality, in its visible appearance; a rigorous perspective construction gives way to a tonal composition.

Did Giorgione's contemporaries immediately realize the revolutionary implications and the formidable consequences of the master's innovation? Was Venice divided, then and there, between the young and the old, between the progressive and the traditional schools? For this was not a normal evolution of taste, from one generation to another, but a sudden crisis.

To answer these questions we must know something of Venice's artistic position at that time.

That Giorgione started the modern manner in the Veneto, as Da Vinci did in Tuscany and Correggio in Lombardy, is clearly stated by Vasari, and there seems to be no reason for disbelieving him. The facts he relates were fairly recent for him, and yet not so recent that he could not see them in a historical perspective. Even allowing for his undeniable partiality of taste, one cannot deny that he was intelligent and a man of subtle judgement. It is also certain that the young elements of Venice now followed Giorgione as fifty years before in Padua they had followed Mantegna. Even Titian, if one accepts what Vasari and Dolce have written, became a convert to the youth from Castelfranco. The traditionalists resisted, but they were not very numerous, and when Giorgione died at a very early age, he had become the idol of Venice, whose taste he had reformed, particularly in the higher spheres of cultured society. This was due not only to the novelty of his content—the themes he chose, the spectacles he invented—but also to his new pictorial language, which had been immediately understood. The famous correspondence between Isabella d'Este and Francesco Albano testifies to the frenzied search for his works by collectors after his death. Giorgione brought a revolution to Venice, but a peaceful and timely one, rich with positive values, and prepared for by remarkable precedents.

Just when young Giorgione, having studied in the Bellinis' workshops, began his own career, an event of paramount importance occurred in Venice: Leonardo da Vinci paid a brief visit to the city in 1500.

Though Vasari does not mention it, this occurrence appears as the probable basis of a whole series of judgements which determine his critical attitude toward the last historical period of Italian painting: that third phase which Vasari calls the modern manner.

We have no records about the relationship between Da Vinci and Giorgione, but it is known that Da Vinci was called to Venice in 1500 by the Signoria for his advice on military matters, and it is extremely probable that he painted while there, or brought with him some paintings or drawings (perhaps the portrait of Isabella d'Este). Granting that the Venetians may not, at the time, have had direct experience with Da Vinci's painting, it seems unreasonable not to presume that Leonardo, who loved discourse, established contact with Venetian artistic circles and discussed professional problems with them, theorizing upon the optical density and upon the confused and hazy quality of distant objects, the optical phenomena, in other words, which he had been studying.

These problems of dispensing with outlines, and of "escaping from the profiles" were, after all, the same as had appealed to Giovanni Bellini, as a reaction against Mantegna's harshness, and induced him to attempt his first experiments in tonality. Da Vinci had solved the problem thanks to his discovery of *sfumato*, this being the exact translation, in pictorial language, of that density of air which in reality envelops all things, reducing to a common visual denominator the opaqueness of the surroundings and the volumes therein contained, the outlines of which disappear in the mass of the atmosphere. Da Vinci made great use of this technique to express the hazy quality of light in the evening hours. This is his "obscurity", a pictorial summary of surroundings, volumes, and dusk. The effect related to distance, the dispensing with outlines are obtained due to the lack of light. A conquest, the price of which is lack of color!

As far as Giorgione's obscurity is concerned, the validity of Vasari's assertion is proven by comparing the *Gypsy and Soldier* (plate 54) to Giovanni Bellini's *Giovanelli' Madonna* in the Accademia, Venice.

One will notice that the chromatic scale of the *Gypsy and Soldier* follows the opposite progression from that of the *Madonna*, in so far as it departs from a basis rich in color and charged with pigment, and therefore comparatively dark in the areas exposed to light, and then moves on to the shadows, where the hues are even deeper and darker. It is as though Bellini's colorful abstractions, the celestial transparencies of this last period, had found the core of a concrete chromatic substance. "Obscurity", therefore, but with a fullness of color at the same time.

That density of the air which Da Vinci the scientist recognized as universal, but which Da Vinci the artist could only express through penumbra, by sacrificing color, is achieved by Giorgione in terms of distance, thereby leaving intact the joy of color.

To represent the near objects as if they were distant, in other words emptied of tangible weight, means to resolve those objects in terms of pure color. But that color is graduated, because there is always, in air, a certain element of shadow blending with light, that veil in the night, which, however thin, will filter into the day. It is a shadow which not only falls on objects and gives them shape, but enfolds them and, in a sense, penetrates them.

At this point the thickening of darkness inside color, while on the one hand inserting into universal vision the evidence and the presence of the nearest objects, on the other reveals the exact measure of distances, so that the objects can be situated in their proper depth.

By these means distance becomes enriched with the closer experience; remoteness acquires propinquity; the substance and structure of things, the knowledge of the world are absorbed into its appearance.

One of the many aspects of this distant vision of Giorgione is the very scant interest shown by him in architectural scenography, which must be seen in "close-up".

We can almost imagine Vasari's patronizing smile as he wrote that to Giorgione's mind "painting directly with colors, without any attempt at preparatory drawing, was the real and the best way of drawing". These words, in fact, are immediately followed by an outburst in praise of drawing. But actually, the technical practice of painting with color alone, which requires the strictest discipline of one's sensitivity, presupposes a very important discovery: that color, while neither ignoring nor neglecting the laws of draftmanship and chiaroscuro, can transcend them, involving them in one single creative act.

It was actually Giorgione's poetic feeling for distance that revealed to him the new language and the best instrument for his aesthetic expression.

Having ascertained that Giorgione's technical interests coincided, at the start, with those of Leonardo, but then rapidly overtook them in a deeper, richer, and more complex interpretation of the world, we must now try to establish a clearer relationship between the two masters.

In 1490 the *Virgin of the Rocks* was completed, and by the beginning of 1498, *The Last Supper* was also completed. These were the years when Giorgione first began his professional activities, of which we know nothing definite. It seems reasonable to assume, aside from the works themselves, that fundamentally he liked to paint with colors alone. At the time of which we are speaking he must already have been so inclined. Da Vinci's arrival in Venice, in 1500, took place at a time when Giorgione, aged twenty-four, must already have shown some distinction, and may certainly have contributed toward throwing a theoretical light upon the technical problems that Giorgione had already solved in practice. Da Vinci's advice, in the author's opinion, should have played a great part in helping the younger painter to clarify his critical thinking and to formulate his own artistic language.

From this meeting Giorgione possibly acquired a greater assurance, a less self-conscious attitude, a bolder determination in his choice of shapes. This particular phase may perhaps have been recorded in the transition from the minute and almost weak compositions, in a style not unlike that of miniatures, rich with little chorus figures, to the more grandly composed works, in which the cast obeys a *mise en scène*. (See the three *Nativities* in plates 25, 30 and 33, and the *Castelfranco Madonna*, plate 42.)

Giorgione's poetic attitude also derived in part from his musical experience. This does not refer to his musical exercises upon which, from Vasari onwards, so many have insisted, and which would still have bound him closer to Da Vinci, but to his participation in musical circles which were particularly active in Venice at that time. Perhaps Raphael may have contributed toward forming his taste through some engravings and drawings of his which were certainly known in Venice at the time. This has been remarked upon by many critics, and Raphael may well have inspired in Giorgione a classically serene and balanced vision of the world. On the other hand, the author cannot accept the many current assumptions that Giorgione was influenced by certain Northern painters and engravers, though it is possible that he occasionally borrowed from them some partial suggestions for motives.

The author also accepts, in principle, Ferriguto's conclusion that Giorgione was greatly interested in the literary culture of his time, though he cannot agree with that author's evaluation of the relationship between Giorgione and Da Vinci.

All these stimuli, and doubtless still others, combine to explain that constant transformation which is true of the life of every artist worthy of that name: life means change, both in the physical and in the material sense. To this constant transformation the artist himself contributes by reacting, positively or negatively, to his stimuli; by his own independent creative impulses; by reflection and exercise; and by the preparation and the execution of his works of art. In Giorgione's case, by training his own sensitivity to perceive, to measure and to define the ever subtler distinctions in chromatic relations.

This continuous inner formation is reflected in the concrete aspects of the work, the line of development of the artist's style, and the history of his artistic life.

Before attempting to trace this line of development, we must go back to that formative period of Giorgione's student days when he was learning both the grammatical and the manual rules of his future profession.

It would appear that his master was Giovanni Bellini, or both the Bellini brothers, or first Gentile, and then Giovanni. The latter is the most obvious version, considering Giambellino's position in Venice at the time when the youth arrived there from the Italian mainland where it is possible that he had learned, in some other workshop, the first rudiments of his craft and given signs of some promise.

Vasari, however, having indicated the goals that Giorgione hoped to achieve by studying and working with the Bellinis, adds immediately, "and by himself", a phrase which is significant.

Returning to the foundation of Giorgione's art, that is to say, to his poetical motive which can be summarized in his concept of distant vision: the pictorial language expressed by that approach and which involves the employment of pure color. This position is a radically new one, at least within the limitation of the artist's cultural experiences.

This new language of pure color seems so relevant, so necessary indeed to the representation of a new world of visual imagery, to the expression of that new poetic feeling, that one must regard it as a revelation to the artist in terms of a sudden illumination, as an idea pregnant with limitless development.

Surely Giorgione, as a boy, must have frequented artists' workshops; these were perhaps mediocre establishments on the mainland. He surely must have seen, in Venice, the works of Giovanni Bellini and have discovered, especially in the twenty-year-old paintings of that master, some latent tendency towards an interpretation of visual appearance very similar to his own. He must also have felt the affectionate humanity of Bellini's art, but let it be said that because of that same confidential tone both psychological and visual, which Bellini brought to his pictures, these contain only partial threads of *rapprochement* to the new use of color alone to express form. The ultimate secret eluded him, and only Giorgione could find it, with his *visione lontana*, the only vision which can reduce the visual world to pure color without a sense of omission.

Note how the two artists represent landscape. In the mature Giambellino it predominates so much that it almost becomes the subject of the painting, as for instance in the *St Francis* (New York, Frick Collection) and in the *Sacred Allegory* (Florence, Uffizi). These two works are magnificent for the fertility of their inventions and for the richness and variety of their episodes, but here and there they betray additions. The display of natural rural beauty by this inhabitant of the lagoon, who must have seen that beauty comparatively late in life, having spent his childhood in his city of stone, between the sky and the water, is equivalent to erudite complacency, so much so that one cannot avoid the feeling of artificiality, as in the case of an anthology of selected passages, which can never unite to form a poem.

From birth, Giorgione, the country lad from the mainland, had seen the great changing sky, tranquil in sunlight or torn asunder by storms over fields and meadows; he had seen the pattern made by the leaves against that sky, and the quiet nooks in the woods under little bridges; he had seen lazy, tortuous brooks weave their way through the grass or along ancient walls; he had seen the rolling hills and the ridged backs of mountains.

These sights, so familiar to mankind, appeared to him as providing the approach to the elemental and natural way of representing the inner essence of everything. They impressed themselves on his mind not so much as outward terms of reference, but as an inner guiding force. And this is why the landscapes, so copiously invented by his imagination—for they are even more imaginative than Giambellino's land-scapes—acquired such an intense and consistent quality of veracity and organic unity, as to appear spontaneously born, even if here and there the single details of his landscapes seem less faithful and more extravagant than those of Bellini. The most poetically fabulous aspects of Giorgione's work are perfectly credible, his dreams are endowed with a most persuasive realism.

Giorgione must also have studied and admired the paintings left in Venice, twenty years before, by Antonello da Messina, whom G. Fiocco considers to have provided the basis for, or certainly the most important stimulus to, the youth's artistic formation. Naturally, as Antonello left Venice at the time of Giorgione's birth, his influence could not have been a direct one. Also this influence was limited in that it could only consist of those aspects of Antonello's art which could appeal to Giorgione's artistic nature: referring specifically to those representations of distances in Antonello's *St Sebastian* and in the Antwerp *Crucifixion*, both admirable works for their balanced broadness, for their transparency and especially for the organized and simple clarity of their construction—this being most probably the legacy of Piero della Francesca.

While Giorgione was painting frescos on the façade of the newly rebuilt Fondaco dei Tedeschi (German Warehouse) in 1507–8, Fra Bartolomeo stayed in Venice, but his influence would appear to have been negligible compared with Giorgione's own study of the Ferrara School, and especially of Costa, Francia, and Benvenuto Tisi (called Garofalo).

Though the influence is undeniable, Giorgione had in Venice itself a much greater source of inspiration. Carpaccio, who would have appealed to him not only because of his similarity of expression, but because of his poetic feeling and tonal vitality.

To sum up this early formative period of Giorgione, the question may be posed whether he was not—as were other painters of his time—a self-taught artist. It is not irreverent, in fact, to call him a dilettante—quickly qualifying that word with, of genius. What is meant is that, with him, the motives behind his personality were stronger than those of his cultural milieu, though he may have been abundantly gifted in other fields, such as literature, music and perhaps even philosophy. Certainly his freedom of expression was never stifled by academicism. Grammar and rhetoric are never set above or against his poetry. This ultimately explains why his art suddenly expanded, as it were, into the fullness of his inspirational energy, achieved force, the *lontananza*, and the absolute of his representational medium—color.

Since it is usual for a young artist to be influenced by his master, it becomes of special interest to discover the point when the embryo of his own personality emerges in his work.

There is a small canvas in the Rasini Collection, in Milan, depicting *Judith* (plate 11), which the author insists upon attributing to the youthful Giorgione. Some parts of the painting definitely appear to be drawn and painted by Cima. This applies to the two women and especially to *Judith* herself. Furthermore, the general composition recalls the two frontal paintings on a chest which Berenson has attributed to Cima. The landscape, on the other hand, reminds one of Bellini. But consider the sense of fantasy, the animation of the invention, and the atmospheric control which conditions the picture's entire development! As compared to Cima's bucolic works, fresh and earthy as they are, we see here the whole spectacle moving away from us, almost out of focus, we feel that the picture's sense of life is melting away into a slow and subtle reverie, that its "story" is being diluted through the landscape into the separate episodes of these absent-minded characters: the heavy sleep of the Turk on the right, and the dialogue on the left between the other Turk and a young man in fashionable clothes. These two are definitely Giorgionesque, and the same might be said of the trees in this picture, with their elastic, vibrating trunks, and also of the plants in the copse seen on the left; this type of flora recalls the vegetation in the two small panels in the Uffizi's *Judgement of Solomon*, and *Trial of Moses* (plates 12 and 13), and also in the *Gypsy and Soldier* (plate 54). The foliage is different from the customary styles of that period, and peculiar to Giorgione. This fusion of obvious contributions by Cima and Giorgione, in a Giorgionesque atmosphere, could easily and simply be explained by the theory that Cima was Giorgione's master. It would not seem unreasonable that the lad from Castelfranco, after his arrival in Venice, chose as his teacher the elderly and reputable artist who not only had come from the mainland like himself, but was actually a native of Conegliano, a town very near Castelfranco. Furthermore, it is worth while noticing that Cima must certainly have been in contact with the Ferrara School, and this could be the explanation for Giorgione's occasional classicist attitudes.

To trace Giorgione's career and to establish the dates of his works is an extremely difficult task for a critic because of the limited knowledge we have of his life and the uncertainty surrounding the authorship of many paintings attributed to him. The very fact that his working life spanned a period of only twelve to fifteen years at the most helps to explain the disconcerting variety of opinions held by critics about Giorgione.

For this reason it becomes necessary to attempt a reconstruction of the painter's inner artistic development with respect to external cultural stimuli on the basis of the few essential elements which we can deduce from those paintings known for certain to be his own, and from the works of experts of high repute, such as L. Venturi, G. Fiocco and A. Morassi. Even so, there is the constant danger of being too subjective and arbitrary in judgement.

After his student debut consisting of the Rasini *Judith*, and after a first experience of mural decoration in which he displayed remarkable gifts of invention (the frescos in the Pelizzari house in Castelfranco, plates 1–10), Giorgione presumably studied the works of Bellini and Antonello, but above all the works of Nature. We can picture him slowly realizing the secret of his own art, becoming more and more fascinated by distance as a fundamental pictorial motive, and discovering pure color as his best means of expression.

At first, his discoveries led him only to a partial representation of distance as a true and proper phenomenon, and he reduced his scene to very small dimensions. The density of his colors insured a tonal richness which balanced the shadows and unified the scene in a comparative darkness from which some very bold and intense new harmonies emerged. While he was still experimenting with color, he gave full rein to a freedom of invention which derived its themes from life, from history and from legends. The foremost works of this period are some small panels, of which two beautiful ones are now in the Padua Museum (plates 16 and 17). In *Leda and the Swan* (plate 16), Leda's rosy flesh stands out between the two whites of the sheet and of the swan, against the green of the bushes and meadows across which flashes the purple gown of the running woman, with her sleeves of bottle-green sparkling with emeralds and amethysts. In the *Pastoral Scene* (plate 17), the amaranthus of the woman's dress contrasts with the yellow shawl around her knees, while the man wears a brick-red doublet and silvery-white hose. These quick flashes of color make the figures stand out against the dark green meadow which fades away into the blue of the sea and then into the lighter blue of the sky.

In the two Uffizi panels, the *Trial of Moses* (plate 13) and the *Judgement of Solomon* (plate 12), Giorgione showed a great independence of invention—the subject of the *Trial* was quite unusual—but somehow did not achieve the same fortunate expressions, the same perfect balance between poetic feeling and pictorial language, as in the Padua masterpieces. The Uffizi works, which still betray an excessive interest in illustration as such, bring up the problem of Giorgione's collaborators. It is a known and obvious fact that in the *Judgement of Solomon* the arid, awkward figures, and the gesture of the ruffian holding the child, are by another, a mediocre, even incompetent hand. In the *Trial of Moses*, according to some critics, Giorgione painted only the left-hand group; to Longhi, only the central figures; and the other figures could be said to recall some unknown painter of the Ferrara School (one is tempted to think of Dosso). In the landscape too some contrasts are noticeable, not so much in style as in quality.

In the author's opinion as far as the *Trial of Moses* is concerned, discrimination is difficult because even though there is a slight difference between the facial peculiarities of the central group and those of the other figures, the standard of both is very high and the styles are similar. As for the landscapes of the two panels (see plates 14 and 15), I would say that they are both equally beautiful and fascinating for their inventiveness, their sincerity, and the romantic lyricism of their inspiration.

G. Fiocco believes Giorgione's collaborator in the *Judgement of Solomon* to have been Giulio Campagnola, because the figure of Moses' mother in the *Trial* is an exact copy from one of Campagnola's frescos in Padua. Morassi, on the other hand, thinks of Giorgione's workshop companion, Catena. Some coincidences of style led the author to accept, as more probable, Fiocco's theory, even though the fact that Giorgione copied a figure from Campagnola does not necessarily prove that they worked together. On other occasions Campagnola copied Giorgione's works.

Similarly, the author would attribute to Campagnola the two panels depicting the *Story of Paris* belonging to Lord Conway and kept in Allington Castle, Maidstone (see plate 104). The small figures are exactly like those in the *Judgement of Solomon*, while the landscapes are merely void and confused commonplaces, entirely lacking in the poetic truth of the two Uffizi panels.

It is more difficult to form an opinion about the Frankfurt *Finding of Romulus and Remus* (plate 101) because of the poor condition of the panel. However, by revealing the painting's preparatory elements, it offers us a precious technical document. Both the figures and the landscape are of a higher quality than those of the *Story of Paris*, so that the work might be placed—though still with reservations— among those paintings by Giorgione in which he chose mythological subjects, sacred themes, or other episodes in order to paint fanciful landscapes around his figures rather than to place his figures in the landscapes. This genre of his was immediately and widely imitated, as shown by the above-mentioned *Story of Paris* and also by Previtali's *Four Stories of Thyrsis and Damon* (plates 102 and 103), purchased in 1937 by the National Gallery, London, as works of Giorgione. The latter certainly painted, as confirmed by

Michiel, *The Finding   Paris*, a fragment of which is in the Budapest Museum. The whole picture is known to us, thanks to a copy by David Teniers the Younger, in Florence. Of *The Finding of Paris* Michiel wrote: "It was among his first works."

Mention should be made here of a small panel in London's National Gallery, *The Adoration of the Magi*, an affectionate, almost intimate, idyll in which the characters, all of modest appearance, are scattered about the scene, contrary to the common practice of impressive choreography. It is interesting to note the resemblance between some of the characters with those on the right side of the *Trial of Moses*.

This must have been painted at the time when Da Vinci's ideas came to enrich Giorgione's experience so that he gradually developed a fuller awareness of his great powers. This period indeed must have seen Giorgione becoming more familiar with terms such as density of air and softening of contours until he found an entirely new vision into which nearness and distance could finally be unified. The *Adoration of the Magi* became, in fact, the starting point of a series of religious works such as the *Holy Family* (plate 30); the so-called *Allendale Nativity* (plate 33), in which one may observe the Leonardesque quality of the flora, and a copy of which is now in Vienna (plate 100); the Leningrad *Judith* (plate 38), and, finally, the *Castelfranco Madonna* (plate 42).

Parallel to these pictures was a series of portraits among which were the Brunswick *Self-portrait* (plate 62), described by Morassi as "one of Giorgione's most Leonardesque works", the *Portrait of a Youth* in Berlin (plate 66), and a series of idealized heads which included young shepherds with arrows, flutes or apples, a *David* (plate 64) and a *Laura* in Vienna (plate 41) dated 1506. Possibly of the same period is the *Portrait of an Old Woman* (color plate IV), perhaps Giorgione's mother; others have described her as "of a revolting realism", but she is definitely a figure of deep sadness, and her face is not devoid of affection.

So far as the two sacred subjects are concerned (plates 30 and 33), the critics are now beginning to ascribe these to Giorgione; there are, in fact, many points of contact between the London *Adoration* and the figures of Mary and Joseph in the *Allendale Nativity*, all standing out against the dark backgrounds of grottos and walls. There is no discussion whatsoever about the attribution of the Berlin *Portrait of a Youth*; though once attributed to Boccacino, the Vienna *Laura* is now widely accepted as an autograph work, thanks to the inscription on the back which tells us that in 1506 Giorgione was a colleague of Vincenzo Catena. The other idealized heads and the *Self-portrait* are more or less recorded in ancient texts, but some of them, perhaps, are copies. The authorship of the *Castelfranco Madonna* is not corroborated by documentary evidence but very few doubts can be raised about it. The probable date of its execution is *circa* 1505.

Though greatly admired, this work has been the subject of considerable criticism in the last twenty-five years. Hourticq, a brilliant scholar and a great art expert, pointed out many errors in the perspective of the painting. On the other hand Cavalcaselle, who was an able draftsman, pronounced the perspective "scientifically correct". Hourticq also criticized the use Giorgione made in this case of the theory of shadow. Others accuse the master of "timidity"; still others dislike the masking of the skyline by what they call the "trick" of that panel of red velvet, and describe the composition as "not organic".

The author would say, on the other hand, that the rigorous pyramidal scheme of the painting gives to the composition a tight central unity and purifies our vision by limiting it to the bare essentials, namely to the area where the majesty of the divine apparition dissolves in human tenderness. There is a well-defined ascent, marked by the three horizontal planes which cut through the pyramid's sides, and by the vertical areas of the throne, mounting up to the Virgin from the cold marble of the floor to the compact warmth of the red drapery, beyond which the free, open landscape surrounds the *Madonna* with an abundance of skylines.

The gentle breath of color lightly caresses this linear composition, so simply and severely geometrical, and imparts a warmth to the vast, still areas, filled only with silence and devoid of all passion. One should speak of reverence, then, rather than of timidity, on the part of the painter, who thus succeeds in passing on to the spectator an immediacy of emotion such as one finds only in true poetry. In fact, would it not really be more apt to pay tribute to Giorgione's courage in composing such a great musical work with so few notes? It does not seem out of place to call the Castelfranco panel one of the purest and most convincing of his masterpieces.

This work was probably followed by *The Three Philosophers* (plate 48), and by the *Gypsy and Soldier* (plate 54). The authorship of both paintings is acknowledged by Michiel. They are both rich with cultural implications and literary meanings, always profoundly transfigured, and both works have given rise to much speculation.

The most probable interpretation of the *Gypsy and Soldier* is by Stefanini, who connects it to the *Hypnerotomachia Poliphili*, though X-rays of the painting have revealed, under the soldier's figure, that of another bathing woman.

As far as *The Three Philosophers* is concerned—and always

assuming that one may give a definite meaning to these works of an essentially poetic nature—one could accept the theory of Ferriguto, who saw in it a reference to the various currents of thought prevailing at the time in Padua, interconnected to a representation of the Magi. Michiel and Berenson state that the work was finished by Sebastiano del Piombo.

These two paintings were executed approximately between 1506 and 1508. Giorgione was still immersing figures into a landscape, but now there seemed to be a new link of affection between the two components. While *The Three Philosophers* is a proof of the master's full ripening as an artist, the *Gypsy and Soldier* too—still attacked by some critics as a timid and disconnected work—shows a more expert handling of the brush, which had now become docile and entirely subservient to each subtle whim of Giorgione's fancy. This could be taken as evidence that between these two paintings and the previous ones some time had elapsed in the painter's brief career.

The years 1507–8 mark the official acknowledgement of Giorgione's prestige with the commission of a picture for the Doge's Palace in Venice (no trace remains of this work) and his employment, with other artists, to decorate with frescos the exterior of the new Fondaco dei Tedeschi, the previous building having been destroyed by fire in 1504. There are many descriptions of this work, but all that is left of it is a Venus, reduced to a few blobs of red paint. Vasari, however, who saw Giorgione's frescos on the Fondaco, wrote that he "thought only of executing fanciful figures which would show his ability. . . . Here is a man, there a woman . . . it is impossible to tell what it all means."

This, in fact, marks the beginning of Giorgione's new manner, his "grand manner", peculiar to the last two years of his life. In the author's view, the painter derived it from the experiences which he underwent while working on the Fondaco frescos and not, as Vasari might appear to suggest in his chapter on Titian, from the reciprocal influence that Giorgone and Titian had upon one another. Nor would it be acceptable that only in 1507 did Giorgione entirely change his taste and his style; in other words, that he did not acquire a new chromatic vision of the world until that year. We have already noted that Giorgione's tendency to paint in pure color was manifest from his very first efforts. Equally, Vasari's story that at the time Giorgione was congratulated for a Symbol of Justice painted by Titian on another side of the Fondaco, and as a result "would not speak to Titian again, and they were no longer friends", is now considered by many as malicious gossip emanating from Titian's idolatrous admirers. These (as stated by D. Phillips in *The Leadership of Giorgione*) "were anxious to exalt their hero at his leader's expense".

It is perfectly admissible, on the other hand, that the fresco practice which is, materially speaking, big, may have broadened Giorgione's pictorial language and thereby helped the development of his final style. Last but not least, one may assume that, to obtain from the Venice Signoria such an important commission as the Fondaco decorations, Giorgione must have previously shown that he had mastered the fresco technique.

The theory of a revolution in Giorgione's painting as opposed to the theory of his development would appear to clash also with Vasari's whole presentation of the master's life which he carefully revised in his second edition of the *Lives*. He omitted from this edition's preamble, for instance, the reference to the *Storm at Sea* (plate 120) which he had first attributed to Giorgione, but he left in it the substance of his parallel between Da Vinci and Giorgione, and particularly the words: "He liked that (Leonardo's) manner so much that he followed it as long as he lived." With regard to those last two years, we should speak of an ascent more than of a turning point, the trail of which had been already blazed by Giorgione's earlier works. Let us finally remember that Bellini, in his *San Zaccaria Altarpiece* (1505), was already Giorgionesque; in fact he was like both Giorgione and Da Vinci.

This is the period which causes the greatest controversy in the attribution of works to Giorgione, to Titian and other followers, especially to Sebastiano del Piombo. The great variety of opinions—some authoritative—proves how difficult it is to feel reasonably sure about any picture, particularly since Michiel informs us that a number of Giorgione's paintings were finished or reconditioned by Titian and Sebastiano. Hourticq has analytically compared the Louvre's *"Concert Champêtre"* (plates 72–73) with one of Titian's drawings in the Malcolm Collection (British Museum) in order to prove that Titian executed both, but his arguments are not entirely convincing. Unfortunately one cannot do more than refer each controversial work, in its more intimate and essential aspects, to one's concept of Giorgione's style, and proceed from there. Such an image, of course, should not be too rigid, but in order to distinguish between Giorgione and Titian, one should look for a line separating breadth from opulence, intensity of contrasts in color from mere chiaroscuro plasticity, and—on the psychological plane—lyricism from dramatization. There is in Giorgione an inner quality of almost virgin immaturity which is so different from Titian's exuberance. Compare, for instance, the Prado *Madonna* (plate 80) with Titian's *Gypsy Madonna* in Vienna, or the Louvre's *"Concert Champêtre"* with

31

the Pitti Palace *Concert* (plate 117), or finally the Dresden *Sleeping Venus* (plate 68) with the nude figure in Titian's *Sacred and Profane Love* in Rome.

The *Portrait of a Man*, also described as the *Terris Portrait* (plate 90), now in San Diego, was most probably painted by Giorgione during the period of which we are writing, as it bears on the back what appears to be the date 1508. The quality of the chiaroscuro recalls Da Vinci's *sfumato*, but unfortunately the picture adds little to our knowledge of Giorgione's work.

The most controversial subjects, so far as attribution is concerned, are the *Sleeping Venus* and the "*Concert Champêtre*". The attribution to Giorgione of the *Venus* was due to Morelli whose enthusiasm, since he identified the picture as the one mentioned by Michiel, is easy to understand. It was an important discovery, but now others have cast new doubts upon it and would ascribe it to Titian. The author believes that the severe innocence of the young woman's body, the musical quality of the lines, the feeling of confident repose as she sleeps alone, surrounded by silence, are typical of Giorgione. Michiel tells us of a Cupid added to the scene by Titian, but later removed, which was just as well as it certainly would have disturbed, by a beginning of action, the integrity of the silence of that solitude. The episode shows the difference in temperament between the two men.

Some would also attribute to Titian the "*Concert Champêtre*" (plates 72–73). But here, too, the connexion between the landscape and those vague, remote figures is so thin as to suggest the hand of Giorgione, perhaps stretched to the utmost of his warmth of atmosphere and generosity of form. The supreme apathy of the figures' expressions and the lack of meaning in their action appear to underline the divine and eternal freedom of poetry. Whatever Titian may have added, Giorgione conceived and executed the *"Concert Champêtre"*. Both Berenson and D. Philipps are agreed that Giorgione alone is in this painting, both in spirit and in substance.

The author is equally convinced, on the other hand, that the *Concert* in the Pitti Palace (plate 117) is by Titian. The nervous hands of the player, full of tension, and his burning eyes, seem to confirm it, as indeed does the picture's whole electric atmosphere. Venturi, however, in his essay of 1954, accepts it as Giorgione's work.

Of the portraits, one might accept Longhi's attribution to Giorgione of the *Double Portrait* in Rome's Palazzo Venezia, with its thoughtful young man in the foreground (plate 89), but not the otherwise beautiful and passionate *Portrait of Antonio Broccardo* in Budapest (plate 106) which remains disturbingly enigmatic. Equally, the calm, relaxed *Knight of Malta* (plate 85) in the Uffizi was painted by Giorgione, but not the *Gattamelata Portrait* (plate 107) tense with energy and perhaps too "dry" in the contours of its round surfaces.

The author would exclude from Giorgione's authorship the *Judgement of Solomon* at Kingston Lacy (plate 114), painted by Sebastiano del Piombo, *Susannah and Daniel* in Glasgow (plate 116), which the author also believes to be by Sebastiano, and the *Sacred Conversation* in Venice (plate 115), probably by Sebastiano but also possibly by a very young Palma. Rejected, too, would be the attribution of the beautiful, but difficult to define, *The Three Ages of Man* in the Pitti Palace (plate 109).

The two heads in Rome's Borghese Gallery (plates 111 and 112) are undoubtedly magnificent, a feat of "bravura", but no more than that; even if they were not painted a century after Giorgione's death, as some would have it, the two canvases would still seem more recent, by a few decades, than the rest of the master's works. And at any rate, how can we believe that Giorgione, in the very last days of his life, should have suddenly succumbed to melodramatic theatricality? Why should he have given up his birthright of self-discipline, of intimacy, of discrimination, for such a display of loud plebeian gaudiness? Admittedly, a genius has the right to change his thoughts and his mood in the course of his career, but we do not have the right to impose such changes upon him when there are no solid grounds for such suspicions.

There are grounds, on the other hand, for attributing to Giorgione a work comparable to the *Sleeping Venus*, and which could mark the ultimate stage in the master's development, as it coincides perfectly with it and with his inspiration. This is the *Warrior with Page*, in the Spanio Collection in Venice (plate 86).

This painting's prestige is proven by the many and ancient copies of it. The one shown in this book, however, the author considers to be an original. The soft atmosphere enveloping the figures does not detract from the splendid brushwork depicting every detail of the shapes, and the subtlest shades of light and color, but always with that discretion which is so typical of Giorgione; a hint here, an allusion there, are sufficient to bring out the correct importance of each detail: the well-polished cuirasse, the scarf of finest veiling, the slits in the boy's doublet, the edges of his cap, the plumes, the strap, the hair. The figures' complexions are extremely warm, and well-harmonized: the bottle-green of the page's sleeve, the plum-colored doublet, the glowing red of his cap against the clouded gray-blue sky.

The most moving elements of this picture are perhaps to be found in the boy's podgy hands and in the loving care which he puts into the unfastening of his master's straps. The latter, as he surveys the operation with his lower lip protruding, indicates, by the disarrangement of his perspiring hair, that his helmet has just been removed. Probably this is a pause during a battle. Observe that, were he well-combed and more magnificently attired, this could be the same man portrayed in the *Knight of Malta* (plate 85). In fact, this knight, too, belongs to the Order, as shown by the cross on his scarf.

Finally, technical affinities exist between this picture and the *Portrait of a Youth* (plate 88), universally attributed to Titian, but I dare to ascribe it to Giorgione. It is hoped that a *Dead Christ* will soon be on view to the public. This painting is described on page 58, note 15.

Such, I think, was Giorgione, the ultimate Giorgione, whose works that I have recalled give us an image that no other painting would confirm. If Giorgione was the inventor of modern painting, then his teaching goes well beyond painting itself. I know that what I am about to say will make both sceptics and intellectual critics smile, but I must say it all the same, in order to try and make contact with the artist's soul and his poetry, now that we have learned to understand his language.

Undoubtedly Giorgione must have had days when he felt tired, bad-tempered, absent-minded, or just indolent. And possibly, in those moments, he may have produced indifferent works, which have been the source of much perplexity to others. But in his moments of inspiration, of that total commitment which is the artist's real morality, works were born of a beauty which will never fade, full as they were of a pure, youthful charm that sets them apart from all the others. They produce the same pleasure which we feel when, walking along a country road, the wind brings to us suddenly, a hundred yards away, the scent of the humble *Olea fragrans* from behind a garden wall.

If there was a form of painting tantamount to a catharsis, this was Giorgione's: a liberation from the weight of matter. His eyes were as clear as the morning, his affections had the innocence of spring, his dreams the limpidness of a pool of water. Let us grant Titian his midday sun, his glow and his summer: Giorgione, by following his lonely individual trial of *lontananza*, of detachment, achieved the classic serenity of the ancient Athenians.

Giorgione, the painter, taught other painters that, beyond the beautiful colors mixed upon their palettes, there is the beauty of color in a work of art. He was undoubtedly a man who knew about carnal love. By the innocence of his work he has taught us that love survives mortal flesh, and only then does it become real love.

BIOGRAPHICAL NOTES

1476–8. Birth of Giorgione. In the first edition of his *Lives of the artists* Vasari writes that Giorgione from "Castelfranco sul Trevisano was born in the year MCCCCLXXVII". In the second edition Vasari changed this date to "1478, when Giovan Mozenigo was Doge of Venice". The biographer adds that Giorgione died of the plague in 1511 at the age of thirty-four. This date cannot be right as other reliable documents confirm that the artist died in 1510. Among these contradictions and inexactitudes it would appear that Vasari's statement in the second edition about Giorgione's birth is the correct one, for Giovanni Mocenigo, as the name is spelled today, was indeed elected Doge in 1478.

1506, JUNE 1. Giorgione shares a workshop with Catena. He paints the *Laura* in Vienna. On the back of the painting is the inscription: "On the first of June 1506 this was executed by the hands of Master Zorzi of Castelf., a colleague of Master Vizenzo Chaena at the request of Master Giacomo. . . ."

1507–8. Works for the Doge's Palace: on August 14, the payment is ordered of a sum of twenty ducats for a *Telero* in the Audience Hall; on January 24, 1508, payment is ordered of twenty-five ducats; on May 23, thirty-five lire and eighteen soldi are to be paid to the architect Giorgio Spavento for a

curtain for the *Telero* in the Audience Hall. The work, which is unknown, was considered to be finished on that last date.

1508. Works for the Fondaco dei Tedeschi: on November 8, the Providers of Salt are instructed to "do justice" to "Mistro Zorzi da Castelfranco" who has stated that he was dissatisfied with the payment received for painting the Fondaco. On December 11, an Arbitration Committee is appointed, including Lazzaro Bastiani, Vittore Carpaccio and Vittore de Matio, to estimate the value of "the paintings on the front of the Fondaco dei Tedeschi, by Mistro Zorzi da Castelfrancho". The work was valued at one hundred and fifty ducats but, with the approval of "the aforementioned Mistro Zorzi", only one hundred and thirty ducats were paid to him.

1508. Painting of the so-called *Terris Portrait*, as recorded in an inscription on the back of the picture.

1510, AUTUMN. Death of Giorgione. On October 23, he had been dead only a short while; on that date Isabella d'Este, Marchioness of Mantua, wrote to the Orator Taddeo Albano, in Venice, instructing him to buy a "painting of a night" (nativity) which should have been among Giorgione's belongings. Albano replied on November 7, that Giorgione "died several days ago of the plague". The plague is recalled also in the diary of Marin Sanudo. It was a particularly virulent one, especially between September 12 and 27. This would confirm Vasari's version of Giorgione's death, though the biographer mistook the year in which it took place. As regards the "painting of a night" mentioned by Isabella, Albano replied that such a picture did not appear among the master's belongings, but added that "Taddeo Contarino owns one, and Vittorio Beccari a better one". However, Albano goes on to say: "neither picture can be bought at any price, because they commissioned them for their own enjoyment".

GIORGIONE'S PAINTINGS

Plate 1

MEDALLION. *Fragment of a fresco, detached from those in the Pellizzari house, shown in the following plates. Castelfranco, Casa Rostirolla.*

Plates 2–6

FRESCOS *in a large room of the Pellizzari house in Castelfranco. Strip (On the north-west wall 156·8 × 75·5, south-east wall 158·3 × 63*).* Strip of yellow tones, with white lights and black shadows, the whole in chiaroscuro: instruments pertaining to the various sciences, medallions, cameos and latin mottos. Cavalcaselle, and later Borenius, were the first to give these frescos serious consideration. Richter, Morassi and Fiocco ascribe them to Giorgione, helped perhaps by some assistant. Such decorations are fairly traditional on the Venetian mainland, both without and within the houses, and they are often entrusted to eminent artists. It is not surprising, therefore, that Giorgione should have had a hand in these frescos, especially as they seem to reveal something of his genius for invention and originality. He was probably very young at the time of their execution, though they may also be dated from a time nearer the painting of the *Castelfranco Madonna* (plate 42). (See also plates 7–10.)

Plates 7–10

FRESCOS *in the Pellizzari house as described above.* Details of medallions,

geographical and astronomical drawings and instruments of the military, musical and representational arts.

Plate 11

JUDITH. *Canvas, 50 × 60. Milan, Rasini Collection.* I believe it to be one of Giorgione's early works. (See page 21.)

Plate 12

JUDGEMENT OF SOLOMON. *Panel, 89 × 12. Florence, Uffizi Gallery.* In 1692, this panel and the next one (*Trial of Moses*) were part of the Grand Duke of Tuscany's collection at Poggio Imperiale. They were also unsigned. In 1793 they were transferred to the Uffizi as works of Giovanni Bellini. Cavalcaselle's attribution of them to Giorgione and his assistants was generally accepted. As to the identity of the assistants, Fiocco suggests Giulio Campagnola for the figures in the *Judgement of Solomon*, and the landscape of the *Trial of Moses*; Morassi thinks Vincenzo Catena contributed to the *Judgement*; Longhi attributes to an unknown artist of the Ferrara School the lateral figures of the *Trial*. This work, in the author's opinion, was carried out almost entirely by Giorgione, whereas in the *Judgement* the artist was responsible for the composition and landscape, and probably left the figures to Campagnola. Whilst the theme of the *Judgement of Solomon* was a fairly common one, the subject of the *Trial of Moses* was

* All dimensions are given in centimeters.

extremely unusual, and was inspired by the Talmud in which it is written that the child Moses, confronted with the choice between a platter laden with jewels and a red hot brazier, chose the latter. (See also plate 14.)

Plate 13

TRIAL OF MOSES. *Panel, 89 × 12. Florence, Uffizi Gallery.* See comment on plate 12. (See also plate 15.)

Plate 14

JUDGEMENT OF SOLOMON. *Florence, Uffizi Gallery.* Detail of landscape.

Plate 15

TRIAL OF MOSES. *Florence, Uffizi Gallery.* Detail of landscape.

Plate 16

LEDA AND THE SWAN. *Small panel, 12 × 19. Padua, Museo Civico.* This panel should be associated with three others shown in plates 17, 18 and 19 (and perhaps with a fifth one kept in the Suardo Collection at Bergamo). The almost perfect coincidence of these panels' dimensions, and the fact that they are all more or less similar in style, suggests the possibility that they may have graced a single piece of furniture, perhaps a small jewel coffer. Indeed they may have come from the house of the Falier family at Asolo and, if it were so, the attribution to Giorgione would be even further corroborated. This *Leda and the Swan*, together with the *Pastoral Scene* (plate 17), comes from the Emo Capodilista Collection. The directors of the Museo Civico attributed them (with some reservations) to Giorgione, but Cook, Lord Conway, Fiocco and Morassi were definite in their attribution;

Justi and Venturi ascribe it to an imitator, others to Campagnola.

Plate 17

PASTORAL SCENE. *Small panel, 12 × 19. Padua, Museo Civico.* See under plate 16. Observe how the arrangement of this scene foreshadows, in terms of theme, that of the *Gypsy and Soldier*.

Plate 18

ALLEGORY OF TIME. *Small panel, 12 × 19. Washington, Phillips Collection.* See what has been written for plate 16. This tablet, attributed by B. Berenson to a "Giorgionesque furniture painter", came originally from the Pulszky Collection in Budapest which consists mainly of pictures from the Veneto; in 1937 it was moved to the St Luke Gallery in Vienna. Later still it was acquired by the Thyssen Collection, Lugano. Many critics agree that it was painted by the same hand as the two Padua tablets (plates 16 and 17).

Plate 19

LANDSCAPE WITH NYMPH AND CUPID. *Small panel, 11 × 20. Washington, National Gallery of Art, Kress Collection.* See under plate 16. The panel comes from the Collection of Count Falier at Castelle d'Asolo and was bought by the Kress Foundation in 1939. Morassi considers the painter to have been Previtali. Others, like de Batz, find in it elements common to the three previous tablets (plates 16, 17 and 18). Berenson dismisses it as, again, the work of "a Giorgionesque furniture painter".

Plate 20

ALLEGORY OF CHASTITY. *Canvas, 28 × 39. Amsterdam, Lanz Collection.* The painting comes from the

Kaufmann Collection where it was attributed to Giorgione, with the endorsement of Bode and Richter. Morassi and Fiocco accept this with reservations. Berenson, Monneret and Justi believe it to be by a Giorgionesque painter. Frizzoni believes it to be a copy.

Plate 21

AENEAS AND ANCHISES. *Canvas, 71 × 90. London, private collection.* This painting comes from the Dona' delle Rose Collection in Venice, acquired in turn from the Villa Garzoni at Ponte Casale in 1933. The attribution to Giorgione is opposed by Lorenzetti who ascribes the canvas to Campagnola. Richter and Morassi reserve their judgement. Fiocco thought at first of Campagnola, then revised his opinion and accepted Giorgione's authorship. G. Sangiorgi (*Illustrated London News*) believes this picture to be the one listed by Michiel, who had seen, in Taddeo Contarini's house, "a large oil painting of Hades, with Aeneas and Anchises". Longhi is definitely in favor of Giorgione. The canvas was not accepted as a work of the Castelfranco master at the time of its export. It had been repainted and restored twice and may have been altered. However, as far as one can tell from photographs, the scenic invention, the structure, the contrast in the landscape between light and shadow—so reminiscent of the *Allendale Nativity* (plate 33) and of *The Three Philosophers* (plate 48)— are so very Giorgionesque, and of such a high quality as to make Longhi's view completely acceptable.

Plate 22a

PARIS ON MOUNT IDA. *Panel, 38 × 56·5. Princeton, University Art Museum, the property of Frank Jewett*

Mather, Jr. Attributed to Giorgione by Professor Mather, Sr., with the endorsement of Lord Conway, Richter, de Batz and Morassi. Fiocco believes it to be the work of an imitator.

Plate 22b

COUNTRY LANDSCAPE. *Panel, 46 × 44. Northampton, Castle Ashby.* Lord Conway and Fiocco attribute it to Giorgione. Berenson disagrees.

Plate 23

THE FINDING OF PARIS. *Canvas, 91 × 63. Budapest Museum.* This is only a fragment of a larger picture —some five feet wide—recalled by Michiel in Taddeo Contarini's house, "the canvas of a landscape with the birth of Paris, and two shepherds standing by". The scene was engraved by Van Kessel in *Theatrum pictorium* in 1659, and copied by Teniers the Younger (see plate 96b). This fragment, showing the two shepherds and a portion of the child's head, is considered an original by Morelli, Justi and others, and with reservations by Morassi. Fiocco is not alone in describing it as a copy. The many repaintings make it very difficult to express an opinion.

Plate 24

MADONNA READING. *Panel, 75·5 × 61. Oxford, Ashmolean Museum.* Detail. Known also as the *Tallard Madonna*, this was part of the Duke of Tallard's Collection in 1756, and was sold as a Cariani at Christies on May 13, 1949, when it was bought by the Ashmolean Museum and acknowledged as a Giorgione by K. T. Parker. The critics were almost unanimous in accepting this attribution, with the exception of

Berenson. Morassi thinks it a late work by the master, datable about 1507–8. The whole picture can be seen in the next plate (color plate I).

Plate 25

ADORATION OF THE MAGI. *Predella panel, 30 × 81. London, National Gallery.* In 1882 this panel was part of the Miles Collection, at Leigh Court, as a work by Giovanni Bellini. It has been in the National Gallery since 1884. Cavalcaselle, Berenson, Justi, Fiocco and Morassi claim that it was painted by Giorgione; A. Venturi sees it as the work of an anonymous Giorgionesque painter; Morelli attributes it to Catena and so does L. Venturi; Richter is doubtful and tends to favor Giorgione but with the participation of Bellini's workshop. This is obviously an early work, closely connected with the Washington *Holy Family* (plate 30). It contains a few odd facial features recalling the *Trial of Moses* (plate 13). The author would connect it with the *Madonna Reading* (color plate I) and with the *Allendale Nativity* reproduced in plates 33–37. (See also plates 26–29.)

Plate 26

ADORATION OF THE MAGI. *London, National Gallery.* Detail of the Virgin and Child.

Plate 27

ADORATION OF THE MAGI. *London, National Gallery.* Detail of St Joseph.

Plate 28

ADORATION OF THE MAGI. *London, National Gallery.* Detail of the Magi.

Plate 29

ADORATION OF THE MAGI. *London, National Gallery.* Detail of two grooms.

Plate 30

HOLY FAMILY. *Panel, 21 × 25. Washington, National Gallery of Art, Kress Collection.* Bought from an antiquarian in 1887 by Henry Willet, it went later to the Benson Collection, London (hence the title of the *Benson Holy Family*); when this collection was dispersed it was acquired by Lord Duveen, who later passed it on to the Kress Collection. It is acknowledged as a Giorgione by H. Cook, Justi, Suida, Berenson, Richter, Morassi and Fiocco. Berenson and L. Venturi had at first thought it a Catena. (See also plates 31 and 32.)

Plate 31

HOLY FAMILY. *Washington, National Gallery of Art.* Detail of central group.

Plate 32

HOLY FAMILY. *Washington, National Gallery of Art.* Detail of landscape in the right-hand background.

Color Plate I

MADONNA READING. *Oxford, Ashmolean Museum.* (See plate 24.)

Plate 33

THE ALLENDALE NATIVITY. *Panel, 91 × 111. Washington, National Gallery of Art, Kress Collection.* Also known as the *Beaumont Adoration.* The Gallery's catalogue states that this may possibly be one of the *Nights* mentioned in the correspondence between Isabella d'Este and her buyer, Taddeo Albano. Morassi accepts this and specifies that in his opinion the painting is the one seen by Albano in Vittorio Beccaro's house. Morassi, however, also admits, though doubtfully, that this painting may be the "creche" evaluated by Paris Bordone in 1563 in the house of Giovanni Grimani, or even a painting which belonged to King James III of England, as stated in the Bathoe Catalogue of 1785. The painting's history can be positively traced from 1841, when Cardinal Fesch's collection was auctioned; it then passed to the Claudio Terral and later to the T. Wentworth Beaumont Collection (1847); Lord Allendale inherited it, and from him, in 1939, through the Duveen brothers, it became the property of the Kress Collection. A drawing at Windsor Castle, mentioned by Cavalcaselle and Dreyfus, is thought by Hadeln, Justi and Parker to be an autograph, whilst Popham and Morassi call it a "derivation".

The Washington panel is traditionally attributed to Giorgione by Cavalcaselle, Cook, Justi, Phillips, Morassi, Fiocco, Longhi and others. Berenson now accepts the attribution but believes the painting to have been completed by Titian. L. Venturi also has now revised his opinion and accepts it as a Giorgione. In Roger Fry's opinion the painter was Cariani; Holmes believes it to be by Bonifazio. The American Gallery's catalogue, and the greater part of the experts who acknowledge the canvas as a Giorgione, consider it an early work dating from about 1500–5. Morassi, however, believes that the master painted it later. (See also plates 34–37, and plate 100a.)

Plate 34

THE ALLENDALE NATIVITY. *Washington, National Gallery of Art.* Detail of St Joseph.

Plate 35

THE ALLENDALE NATIVITY. *Washington, National Gallery of Art.* Detail of the Virgin.

Plate 36

THE ALLENDALE NATIVITY. *Washington, National Gallery of Art.* Detail of the shepherds.

Plate 37

THE ALLENDALE NATIVITY. *Washington, National Gallery of Art.* Detail of the landscape in the left-hand background.

Plate 38

JUDITH. *Panel transferred to canvas in 1838. Leningrad, Hermitage Museum.* The picture's measurements were reduced, between 1755 and 1770, to 144 × 65; about 13 cm. were cut from each side. The panel was taken from Italy to France towards the end of 1600, and passed from one collection to the other (Bertin, Pierre Crozat in 1729, Louis Francois Crozat, Baron of Thiers, in 1740); while in the Baron's possession it was made the subject of an engraving, as a Raphael, by Toinette Larcher (*Recueil d'estampes . . . ,* Paris, 1729–42) and listed in its original dimensions in 1755; it was seen and cut down to its present measurements by Saint-Aubin in 1770. In 1772 Catherine II of Russia bought it, together with the whole Crozat Collection, for the Hermitage Museum. Following Larcher's engraving, the panel continued to be ascribed to Raphael until, in 1864, Waagen suggested to Morelli, who still remained uncertain, Giorgione. This is now almost universally accepted. (See also plate 39.)

Plate 39

JUDITH. *Leningrad, Hermitage Museum*. Detail of Judith's face.

Plate 40

PORTRAIT OF A LADY. *Canvas, 31·7 × 24·1. New York, Duveen Brothers*. Formerly the property of Prince Lichnowsky at Kuchelna (Czechoslovakia), and later of Lord Melchett at Romsey, Hampshire. The attribution to Giorgione is accepted by Berenson, Gronau, Richter, Tietze, Richardson and de Batz. The resemblance to *Laura* (see plate 41) leads the author to share this view.

Plate 41

PORTRAIT OF LAURA. *Canvas attached to panel, 41 × 33·6. Vienna, Kunsthistorisches Museum*. Formerly in the Gallery of Archduke Leopold Wilhelm in Brussels, as shown in an inventory of 1659. Later in Vienna as part of the Imperial Collections. The painting has been attributed alternatively to Bassano, to Palma's school, to Romanino (by Engerth in 1883), and to Boccaccino by A. Venturi. In 1908 Justi, on the basis of the reading by Dollmayr of an inscription on the back of the picture, attributed it with some hesitation to Giorgione. Later he was supported almost unanimously by Longhi, Hourticq, Wilde, Hermanin, Fiocco, Morassi and Berenson. Only Richter remains doubtful.

Plate 42

MADONNA WITH SS FRANCIS AND LIBERALE. *Panel, 200 × 152. Castelfranco, Church of San Liberale*. This famous altarpiece, many times arbitrarily restored, was retouched once again in 1938 by Mauro Pellicioli, who also restored Da Vinci's *Last Supper*. Pellicioli consolidated the colors, but conscientiously returned to their original state all the parts which had been altered by his predecessors. For some critics, including Hourticq, the knight at left (plate 46) is St George, but there really seems to be no doubt whatsoever that it is St Liberale. The attribution to Giorgione was first made by Ridolfi who visited Castelfranco in 1640 and talked to the locals. He did not, however, state his opinion until 1684. Since then no one has disputed the authorship, though the date of execution is still a subject of discussion. Gronau and Richter, knowing that the altarpiece was intended for the Costanzo family chapel, believed that it was painted before 1504, the year of young Matteo Costanzo's death. More reasonably, others claim that the work was executed immediately after that date, by order of Matteo's father, the Condottieri Tuzio Costanzo, in memory of his son.

While the painting is generally considered one of the world's great masterpieces, Hourticq is rather critical of it and calls it "this Madone stylithe". Longhi too finds it far from perfect, pointing out here and there signs of uncertainty, of timidity, even of awkwardness. In a recent essay, however, L. Venturi proclaims once again the altarpiece's great merits.

Plate 43

MADONNA WITH SS FRANCIS AND LIBERALE. *Castelfranco, Church of San Liberale*. Detail of the Virgin and Child.

Plate 44

MADONNA WITH SS FRANCIS AND LIBERALE. *Castelfranco, Church of San Liberale*. Detail of the left-hand landscape.

Plate 45

MADONNA WITH SS FRANCIS AND LIBERALE. *Castelfranco, Church of San Liberale*. Detail of the right-hand landscape.

Plate 46

MADONNA WITH SS FRANCIS AND LIBERALE. *Castelfranco, Church of San Liberale*. Detail of St Liberale.

Plate 47

MAN IN ARMOR. *Panel, 39 × 27. London, National Gallery*. Study for the St Liberale in the Castelfranco altarpiece. On the panel is an ancient inscription with the name Giorgione. This was formerly believed to be a portrait of Gaston de Foix, possibly the same de Foix of Lord Bessborough's Collection and of the Smith Collection, both attributed to Giorgione. The painting is certainly identifiable with the Smith knight shown in 1816 and transferred in 1820 to the Rogers Collection. It was donated to the National Gallery in 1855. First attributed to Giorgione by Cavalcaselle and now by Morassi. Fiocco calls it a derivation.

Plate 48

THE THREE PHILOSOPHERS. *Canvas, 121 × 141·5. Vienna, Kunsthistorisches Museum*. This canvas, which has been cut down, especially on the left-hand side, is one of the very few paintings definitely by Giorgione. It was, in fact, minutely described by Michiel, who had seen it in 1525 in Taddeo Contarini's house. In 1659 it was quoted in the inventory of Archduke Leopold Wilhelm's Gallery; a year later it was engraved by Teniers; it later went to the Austrian Imperial Collections. Roentgen rays have revealed some departures from the original plans, especially in the head-dress of the old philosopher on the right, who at first wore a diadem, or a fan-like crest. Many interpretations have been offered of this theme: Mechel, in his Catalogue of 1783, speaks of the "Three Wise Men", a title which has been taken up again, in modern times, by Wilde, Wisler and others; Wickhoff, in 1895, saw in the subject Evander and Pallas showing Aeneas the site of the future Capitol; Ferriguto, in 1933, suggested that each of the three figures symbolized the philosophical trends of Giorgione's days: the old man is the Aristotelian school, the figure in the turban is Averroism, while the seated youth represents the new naturalistic science then fashionable in Padua. The fact that the painting was finished by Sebastiano del Piombo, as Michiel himself tells us, does not necessarily mean that Giorgione painted it just before his death. It could have been executed some years before and left unfinished. (See also color plate II and plates 49–53.)

Color Plate II

THE THREE PHILOSOPHERS. *Vienna, Kunsthistorisches Museum*. Detail of the three figures.

Plate 49

THE THREE PHILOSOPHERS. *Vienna, Kunsthistorisches Museum*. Detail of trees and landscape.

Plate 50

THE THREE PHILOSOPHERS. *Vienna, Kunsthistorisches Museum*. Detail of central landscape.

Plate 51

THE THREE PHILOSOPHERS. *Vienna, Kunsthistorisches Museum*. Detail of the young philosopher.

Plate 52

THE THREE PHILOSOPHERS. *Vienna, Kunsthistorisches Museum*. Detail of the "Eastern" philosopher.

Plate 53

THE THREE PHILOSOPHERS. *Vienna, Kunsthistorisches Museum*. Detail of the old philosopher.

Plate 54

GYPSY AND SOLDIER. *Canvas, 78 × 72. Venice, Gallerie dell' Accademia*. Also recorded by Michiel who had seen it in 1530 in the house of Gabriele Vendramin. The canvas was still there in 1569 as indicated in an inventory of that year. In 1856, under the title of *Mercury and Isis*, it appeared in the Manfrin Gallery; Prince Giovanelli bought it in 1875, and since 1932 it has hung in the Venice Accademia. X-rays have revealed, under the soldier's figure, an earlier outline of a bathing woman (plate 57). Among the many and partly extravagant explanations of the theme, which must have appeared obscure to Giorgione's contemporaries (see Michiel), Stefanini's theory is perhaps most acceptable: he believes the canvas to have been inspired by the *Hypnerotomachia Poliphili*. There is disagreement about the date of execution. Cook thinks the canvas was painted before 1500; Conti and Borenius claim that it preceded the Castelfranco altarpiece; the majority of the others believe it to have been painted later. (See also color plate III and plates 55–60.)

Plate 55

GYPSY AND SOLDIER. *Venice, Gallerie dell' Accademia*. Detail of the woman and child.

Plate 56

GYPSY AND SOLDIER. *Venice, Gallerie dell' Accademia*. Detail of the soldier.

Color Plate III

GYPSY AND SOLDIER. *Venice, Gallerie dell' Accademia*. Detail of background, with landscape and sky.

Plate 57

GYPSY AND SOLDIER. *Venice, Gallerie dell' Accademia*. X-ray of the lower left-hand quarter showing the original figure of the bathing woman, later replaced by the soldier.

Plate 58

GYPSY AND SOLDIER. *Venice, Gallerie dell' Accademia*. Detail of soldier's head.

Plate 59

GYPSY AND SOLDIER. *Venice, Gallerie dell' Accademia*. Detail of woman's head.

Plate 60

GYPSY AND SOLDIER. *Venice, Gallerie dell' Accademia*. Detail of landscape.

Plate 61

PORTRAIT OF AN OLD WOMAN. *Venice, Gallerie dell' Accademia*. Detail of head.

Plate 62

SELF-PORTRAIT. *Canvas, 52 × 43. Brunswick, Herzog Anton Ulrich Museum*. This could be the same self-portrait seen by Vasari in the house of Grimani, Patriarch of Aquileia and from which he sketched the portrait of Giorgione shown in his biography. Hollar made an engraving of the canvas in 1650, when it was part of the van Verle Collection in Antwerp; in 1737 it was acquired by the Duke of Brunswick and recorded in a 1776 inventory as a self-portrait of Raphael; later it was described as by Dosso Dossi. The picture must have been cut down after 1650. Attributed to Giorgione by Justi, and then by Wickhoff, Hermanin, Richter, Fiocco and Morassi. For L. Venturi and others it is a copy; for Berenson a "version of Giorgione's self-portrait as David" by the elder Palma.

Plate 63

YOUTH HOLDING ARROW. *Panel, 48 × 42. Vienna, Kunsthistorisches Museum*. In 1663 this painting could be seen as an Andrea del Sarto, in Ambras Castle at Innsbruck where it had arrived from Archduke Sigismund's Collection; from 1773 it was part of the Vienna Imperial Collections; ten years later it was listed as a Schedone in Mechel's Catalogue; in 1837 Kraft's Catalogue described it as "Correggio's School". Reasonably, Ludwig identified it with the painting seen by Michiel in Giovanni Ram's house in 1531, and in the home of Antonio Pasqualino a year later. Ram had kept a copy of it which he still believed to be an original. This proves that, even shortly after Giorgione's death there was some uncertainty about this panel, and helps to explain the diverse opinions about it. The Vienna panel is believed to be the original one by Ludwig, Wickhoff, Fiocco, Morassi and Berenson; Gronau and L. Venturi see it as a copy; Mundler and Waagen ascribe it to Bernardino Gatti; Buschbeck to Lotto; Richter and Wilde are doubtful. The fine quality of the picture leads the author to accept it as the work of Giorgione.

Plate 64

DAVID WITH HEAD OF GOLIATH. *Panel, 65 × 74.5. Vienna, Kunsthistorisches Museum*. Formerly part of Archduke Leopold Wilhelm's Collection and engraved in 1660 by Teniers. Attributed by Wilde to an imitator, and by Morassi to Giorgione, although doubtfully, owing to the poor condition of the painting. The panel should find a place among the group of pictures previously discussed, which must also have included the original *Page*, of which plate 98 reproduces only a copy. This David cannot be identified with the *Self-portrait* (plate 62), because of the obvious youth of the figure.

Color Plate IV

PORTRAIT OF AN OLD WOMAN. *Canvas, 69 × 60. Venice, Gallerie dell' Accademia*. As the Vendramin coat of arms appears on the ancient frame, it is reasonable to identify this canvas with the one recorded in that family's inventory of 1569, "the portrait of Giorgione's mother, in the master's own hand, provided by him and adorned with the Vendramin heraldic arms". Later the painting passed to the Manfrin Gallery. It was first attributed to Giorgione by A. Della Rovere in 1903; Monneret, Berenson, Suida, Fiocco and Morassi are among the many who agree. Dates from about the same time as the *Gypsy and Soldier*.

Plate 65

PORTRAIT OF SHEPHERD WITH PIPE. *Canvas, 61 × 51. Hampton Court, Royal Gallery*. Acquired by King Charles I as a Giorgione, it was transferred in 1649 to the de Critz Collection, and in 1688 to King James II's Collection. In 1714 the canvas became part of Queen Anne's Collection and from that time onwards it has remained the property of the British Royal Family. The majority of modern critics agree with Morelli's original attribution to Giorgione. This is certainly true of Wickhoff, Monneret, Gronau, Berenson, Suida; Fiocco, Richter and Morassi reserve their judgement; Cook and L. Venturi ascribe the canvas to Torbido. Rather than a copy or an imitation, the author believes it to be an original variation of the *Youth holding arrow* (plate 63).

Plate 66

PORTRAIT OF A YOUTH. *Canvas, 58 × 46. Berlin, Kaiser Friedrich Museum.* Originally bought in 1884 from the Giustiniani Collection in Padua by Jean Paul Richter who in 1891 sold it to the Berlin Museum. Wickhoff attributes it to Sebastiano del Piombo, but all the others agree that it is by Giorgione. The two letters V.V. on the parapet have yet to be explained; they were probably the initials of the unknown young man. (See also plate 67.)

Plate 67

PORTRAIT OF A YOUTH. *Berlin, Kaiser Friedrich Museum.* Detail of head.

Plate 68

SLEEPING VENUS. *Canvas (transferred from the original in 1843), 108·5 × 175. Dresden, Gemäldegalerie.* Bought, in 1697, on behalf of King Augustus of Saxony by C. le Roy, a merchant. It appeared in a catalogue of 1707 as a Giorgione, but from 1722 onward it was listed as a Titian. Cleaning operations carried out in 1843 brought to light a Cupid which had been previously covered with paint. Owing to the poor condition of this detail, it was decided to cover it again. In 1880 Morelli identified this Venus with the one seen by Michiel in the home of Gerolamo Marcello. In the painting mentioned by Michiel the landscape and the Cupid had been finished by Titian. The experts accepted unanimously Morelli's attribution until, in 1919, Hourticq reduced his acknowledgement of Giorgione's direct participation to the face alone, and in 1930 pronounced himself entirely in favor of Titian. This radically negative position appealed also to Suida, who sought further evidence: (1) a document published by Fogolari about a Giorgione picture seen in the Marcello house in 1730, that is, when the *Sleeping Venus* was already in Dresden (this does not prove that the Giorgione mentioned in the document was the *Venus*); (2) some lines by the poet Boschini alluding to a different position of Venus, but which may equally apply to the Dresden painting. Morassi sides entirely with Hourticq and Suida, though he accepts the spirit of the painting as Giorgionesque, and admits that it is thanks to Giorgione that "such a pure and classical beauty has matured in Titian's art". In his opinion Titian painted this canvas at the time of his *Sacred and Profane Love.*

But, in more recent literature, critics such as Berenson, Fiocco, Longhi, L. Venturi and Gamba favor Giorgione. (See also plates 69, 70 and 71.)

Plate 69

SLEEPING VENUS. *Dresden, Gemäldegalerie.* Detail of Venus.

Plate 70

SLEEPING VENUS. *Dresden, Gemäldegalerie.* Detail of drapery.

Plate 71

SLEEPING VENUS. *Dresden, Gemälde-galerie*. Detail of the head.

Plate 72–73

"CONCERT CHAMPÊTRE". *Canvas, 110 × 138. Paris, Louvre*. Up to 1627 this picture was part of the Duke of Mantua's collection and perhaps, as Justi wrote, it may have belonged to Isabella d'Este. Later it became the property of King Charles I of England, then of the banker Jabach who sold it to Louis XIV of France. Its traditional attribution to Giorgione was contested first by Waagen, who saw it as the work of Palma the Elder, then by Lafenestre and Springer, who suggested Titian, and later still especially by Cavalcaselle, who ascribed it to an imitator of Sebastiano del Piombo. Morelli fought back for Giorgione, with the support of A. and L. Venturi, Berenson, Justi, a converted Gronau, Cook, Richter and Fiocco; but Hourticq, reinforced by Suida and Morassi, insists upon Titian who, in his opinion, began this work immediately after the Padua frescos (1511–12) but did not finish it until after 1530.

Hourticq went so far as to identify this picture with a painting of nudes which Albano, in his letters to Isabella d'Este, stated had been commissioned from Titian. However, the date of 1530 would seem to be too late. Morassi thinks that the *"Concert Champêtre"* was born in the same creative climate as the *Sleeping Venus*, perhaps a few years before. The attribution to Titian is accepted by Longhi. For the majority of critics who ascribe it to Giorgione this picture was painted after the *Sleeping Venus* and constitutes one of the last and most mature achievements of Giorgione. (See also plates 74–79.)

Plate 74

"CONCERT CHAMPÊTRE". *Paris, Louvre*. Detail of the woman on the left (upper part).

Plate 75

"CONCERT CHAMPÊTRE". *Paris, Louvre*. Detail of the woman on the right and of the man in the center.

Plate 76

"CONCERT CHAMPÊTRE". *Paris, Louvre*. Detail of the woman on the left (lower part).

Plate 77

"CONCERT CHAMPÊTRE". *Paris, Louvre*. Detail of the right-hand background: shepherd and flock.

Plate 78

"CONCERT CHAMPÊTRE". *Paris, Louvre*. Detail of the lute player.

Plate 79

"CONCERT CHAMPÊTRE". *Paris, Louvre*. Detail of the central background landscape.

Plate 80

MADONNA WITH SS ANTHONY OF PADUA AND ROCH. *Canvas, 92 × 133. Madrid, Prado Museum*. In or about 1650 this canvas was offered to Philip IV of Spain by the Viceroy of Naples, the Duke of Medina. Velazquez attributed it to Pordenone, Cavalcaselle to Francesco Vecellio, Schmidt to Titian. This last theory is obviously supported by those critics who believe that Titian painted the *Sleeping Venus* (see under plate 68) with the exception of L. Venturi. Morelli and his followers, and now also Gamba, are in favor of Giorgione. (See also plate 81.)

49

Plate 81

MADONNA WITH SS ANTHONY OF PADUA AND ROCH. *Madrid, Prado Museum.* Detail of the central group and St Roch.

Plate 82

CHRIST CARRYING THE CROSS. *Panel, 50 × 39. Boston (Mass.), Gardner Museum.* This panel comes from the Loschi Dal Verme Collection in Vicenza. It is generally attributed to Giorgione. Berenson qualifies: Giorgione after Giovanni Bellini, an early work; Morassi identifies it with Bellini's school, with which there certainly are similarities. A number of copies of this painting are in existence.

Plate 83

CHRIST WITH CROSS AND OTHER FIGURES. *Canvas, 70 × 100. Venice, Church of San Rocco.* The painting has been in San Rocco since it was painted. Michiel recalls, in 1552, in Antonio Pasqualino's house, a *Head of St James* by Giorgione or a pupil, taken from the *Christ of San Rocho.* It would seem reasonable, therefore, to argue that the figure of Christ was also by Giorgione—to whom Vasari attributes it in both editions of his *Lives.* But then Vasari also attributes it to Titian (in his biography of that artist), adding that "Many have thought this to be a work by Giorgione." Venturi explains the mistake by recalling that in San Rocco there is also an *Ecce homo* by Titian. To sum up, we are faced here with differences of opinion the weight of which is not easy to evaluate, for though one tends, as a rule, to accept Michiel's testimony against all others, it may well be that Vasari, in his *Life of Titian,* intended to correct himself on the basis of direct information.

Ridolfi, Boschini, and Sansovino accept the Titian authorship on the strength of Vasari's statement. The work being damaged, it is almost impossible to reach a conclusion, but the contained drama of the scene and the discipline of the attitudes would appear to indicate Giorgione as the painter. Hourticq's comparison of the head of this Christ with the Christ of the *Tribute-money* formerly in Dresden is not convincing. Cavalcaselle favors Giorgione, and so do Berenson and L. Venturi; Hourticq, Suida, Morassi and Pallucchini favor Titian. (See also plate 84.)

Plate 84

CHRIST WITH CROSS AND OTHER FIGURES. *Venice, Church of San Rocco.* Detail of the head of Christ.

Plate 85

KNIGHT OF MALTA. *Canvas, 80 × 64. Florence, Uffizi Gallery.* Formerly part of Paolo del Sera's Collection, from which, in 1654, it passed to the Medici family. Originally ascribed to Titian. Cavalcaselle attributes it to a Giorgionesque painter, Hourticq, Suida and Morassi to Titian. The majority of modern critics accept it as a Giorgione.

Plate 86

WARRIOR WITH PAGE. *Canvas, 70 × 86·5. Venice, Spanio Collection. From the Van Axel Palace Collections; previously the property of Sebastiano Barozzi.* This could be the original of a composition which was copied many times, and ought to be considered, in the author's view, one of the last and most mature works by Giorgione. This opinion is shared by Fiocco and Pallucchini, but others do not agree. Cavalcaselle, in 1871, recalled five different facsimiles of this composition, though in smaller dimensions and without the knight's helmet on the window-sill: (1) in the storage rooms of the Vienna Kunsthistorisches Museum; (2) in the Alfieri di Sostegno home in Turin; (3) in the Carlisle Collection in Naworth Castle, from the Orleans Collections; (4) in Stuttgart's Gallery; (5) a copy signed by G. Pencz in Berlin's Redern Collection. The Naworth Castle replica (now in the Howard Collection in Howard Castle), which could be an original, was reproduced by Richter; the Stuttgart copy, thought by Cavalcaselle to be a more recent copy, was found, when X-rayed, to be superimposed on a *Pieta*, dating from the first half of the sixteenth century, and was therefore eliminated; the Pencz facsimile went later to the Kaufmann Collection.

Plate 87

WARRIOR WITH PAGE. *Venice, Spanio Collection*. Detail of page.

Plate 88

PORTRAIT OF A YOUTH. *Canvas, 80·6 × 69·5. New York, Frick Collection*. Commonly attributed to Titian. Morassi claims that the similarity of style between this picture and the "*Concert Champêtre*" makes it obvious that the same artist painted both works. This is true, and the author would link with these two paintings the *Warrior with Page* (plate 86). But if one attributes to Giorgione, the "*Concert Champêtre*" and the *Warrior with Page*, then one cannot but attribute to him this portrait too, which the author consider his masterpiece in the particular field of portrait-painting.

Plate 89

DOUBLE PORTRAIT. *Canvas, 80 × 67·5. Rome, Palazzo Venezia Gallery*. Ravaglia believes the two young men to be the musicians, Verdelot and Obreth. This painting has been attributed by some to Sebastiano del Piombo. Pallucchini disagrees. Fiocco sees it as a Mancini. The attribution to Giorgione is due to Longhi, and it seems acceptable if one compares this canvas with the *Portrait of a Man* (plate 90).

Plate 90

PORTRAIT OF A MAN. *Panel, 30 × 26. San Diego, California, Fine Arts Society*. Formerly in the Currov and Terris Collections and therefore also known as the *Terris Portrait*. It bears, on the back, an ancient inscription with a date which could be read as 1508. Richter was the first to publish this canvas as a Giorgione, and Gronau, Hadeln, Suida, Fiocco Morassi and L. Venturi agree. (See also plate 91.)

Plate 91

PORTRAIT OF A MAN. *San Diego, Fine Arts Society*. Detail of the face.

Plate 92

VIEW OF CASTELFRANCO. *Red chalk on paper, 20 × 29. Rotterdam, Boymans Museum*. Until 1707 in the Resta Collection, then in the Robinson, Buhler and Koenigs Collection, later in Rotterdam's Boymans. Unanimously accepted as a Giorgione, but with reservations by Justi.

Plate 93a

THE VIOLA PLAYER. *Ink on paper, 19·4 × 14·6. Paris, École des Beaux-Arts*. Formerly in the Cosway and Mayor Collections. Kristeller believes it to be by Campagnola and some ascribe it to Titian, but the majority of modern critics (Hadeln, Justi, Suida, Fiocco, Morassi) attribute it to Giorgione.

Plate 93b

HEAD OF AN OLD MAN. *Paris, École des Beaux-Arts.* Drawing, originally believed to be by Perugino, but attributed to Giorgione by L. Venturi, who considers it a study for *The Three Philosophers*, and, with doubts, by Morassi.

Plates 94 and 95

FRAGMENT OF NUDE. *Fresco, approximately 250 × 140. Venice, Gallerie dell' Accademia.* This is one of Giorgione's frescos on the façade of the Fondaco dei Tedeschi in Venice. It was detached and restored in 1937 by Mauro Pellicioli. This is the only autograph evidence of those frescos, which included many male and female figures, mentioned by a number of eye-witnesses, and copied and engraved by A. M. Zanetti in his book, *Frescos by the most eminent Venetian Masters* (Venice, 1760), from which the reproductions on plates 94b and 95 are taken. Plate 94a shows the damaged fresco discussed in this context.

Plate 96a

THE HOROSCOPE. *Panel, 132 × 192. Dresden, Gemäldegalerie.* Originally considered a Giorgione, later described as a copy by Morelli, supported by A. Venturi, Berenson and practically all modern critics. L. Venturi and Swarzensky, for their part, claim that Giorgione has nothing to do even with this painting's original.

Plate 96b

THE FINDING OF PARIS. *Canvas, 20 × 30. Florence, Loeser Collection.* A copy, by David Teniers the Younger, of Giorgione's lost *Finding of Paris,* a fragment of which is shown in plate 23.

Plate 97a and b

JUDGEMENT OF PARIS. *Two canvases; 52·5 × 67·5 and 60 × 74. Dresden, Gemäldegalerie; Chiavari (Italy), Lanfranchi Collection.* Both copies of an original, now lost, recalled as a Giorgione by Ridolfi. Gronau and Hadeln believe that Domenico Campagnola painted the original; L. Venturi ascribes it to a late imitator; in Morassi's opinion the original was by Titian. Other copies of the same painting are to be found in Oslo's Larpendt Collection, at Malmesbury and in the Uffizi. Andrea Vendramin was the owner of yet another version. It is a fact that Paris was one of Giorgione's favorite subjects. (See also plates 104a and b.)

Plate 98

PAGE. *Panel, 23 × 30. Milan, Pinacoteca Ambrosiana.* Formerly in Cardinal Borromeo's Collection, it was donated to the Ambrosiana in 1618. The original title of the panel was *The Savior as a boy, playing with a ball,* and the painter was believed to be Andrea del Sarto. The work was later attributed to Giorgione and, by Fiocco, to Domenico Mancini. Wilde thought the subject to be Paris with the golden apple. Probably an ancient copy of a work by Giorgione.

PAINTINGS ATTRIBUTED TO GIORGIONE

Plate 99

HOMAGE TO A POET. *Panel, 59 × 48. London, National Gallery.* Formerly in the Aldobrandini and Bohn Collections, under the title *Solomon and his servants*; sold to the National Gallery in 1885. A. Venturi, having first attributed it to Giorgione, revised his opinion, and so did Cook, Justi, and the majority of other critics. Morassi sees this panel as "very closely connected with Giorgione". In fact, though here and there some aridity and triteness of treatment (such as the poet's laurels), may suggest the workshop's intervention, other aspects, such as the beautiful figure of the lute player, reveal the master's hand. Surely Giorgione was also responsible for the invention and the arrangement of masses.

Plate 100a

NATIVITY. *Panel, 91 × 115. Vienna, Kunsthistorisches Museum.* In Archduke Leopold Wilhelm's Collections in 1659 as a Giorgione. This is a replica, with some variations of landscape and in the trees seen on the left, of the *Allendale Nativity* (plate 33). For Fiocco it is the work of Giorgione but completed by others. Morassi sees in it an element of "tiredness" and believes that if the Allendale picture was one and the same as the *Night* of Vittorio Beccaro, this may be the other version seen in Taddeo Contarini's house.

Plate 100b

CERES. *Panel transferred to canvas, 70 × 54. Berlin, Kaiser Friedrich Museum.* In a recent paper, *Berliner Museen*, Zimmermann attributes this work to Giorgione, but his arguments are very disputable. Pallucchini insisted, verbally, on Sebastiano del Piombo. A comparison with the *Small nude* in Vienna, signed by Gerolamo da Treviso the Younger, might support the theory that this artist painted the original panel.

Plate 101

THE FINDING OF ROMULUS AND REMUS. *Panel, 69 × 121·5. Frankfurt, Staedel Institute.* Swarzensky discovered this panel in 1937, and Schwarzweller repainted it after a cleaning operation which damaged it considerably. The work, however, was unfinished, as revealed by the complexions of the faces, which leave bare the drawing underneath. The finished parts are the tree branches and leaves. Swarzensky attributed the panel to Giorgione, and the Gallery's Directors still accept the authorship. Richter is rather in favor of Giorgione's school, Fiocco of Campagnola and Morassi of Catena. Among the many landscapes with small figures comparable to the *Judgement of Solomon* and the *Trial of Moses* (plates 12 and 13), this is probably the best one and should also be compared with the Rasini *Judith* (plate 11). Similar but of a much lower standard, is the

Landscape with small figures, attributed to Giorgione by Morassi.

Plates 102–103

FOUR STORIES OF THYRSIS AND DAMON. *Two small panels, 45·5 × 20, each depicting two stories. London, National Gallery.* Bought in 1937 and attributed to Giorgione by Sir Kenneth Clark. Later ascribed by Borenius to Palma. Richter is supported by the great majority in attributing the panels to Previtali.

Plate 104

STORY OF PARIS. *Two small panels, each 45 × 66. Maidstone, Allington Castle, property of the heirs to Lord Conway.* These were formerly in the Albarelli Collection at Verona, from which they passed to the Duke of Ossuna, then to a merchant in St Jean-du-Luz and finally to Lord Conway. Cook thought them to be by Giorgione and his attribution was accepted by Monneret de Villard and later by Swarzensky and Schwarzweller, connecting them with the *Finding of Romulus and Remus* (plate 101). Lord Conway believes in Giorgione's authorship, but Gronau and Morassi attribute the panels to Catena, L. Venturi to a pupil of Lazzaro Bastiani, and Fiocco, rightly so, to Giulio Campagnola.

Plate 105

PORTRAIT OF GIOVANNI ONIGO. *Canvas, 68 × 55. Richmond, Cook Collection.* Formerly owned by the Onigo family in Treviso, later by the Florentine antique merchant, Volpi. In the Cook Collection since 1907. Attributed to Cariani by Borenius and Morassi, and, correctly, to Pordenone by Fiocco.

Plate 106

PORTRAIT OF ANTONIO BROC-CARDO. (More probably of Vittore Cappello). *Canvas, 72·5 × 54. Budapest Museum.* The faded inscription on the parapet reads: "Antonius Brokardus Marii f.", and is not original. The canvas comes from the collection of the Patriarch of Venice, Ladislao Pyrker, where it was described as a Titian. It is also attributed to Titian by Pulszky. Mündler describes it as by Francesco Morone; Frizzoni, as by Torbido; Ludwig, A. Venturi and Fabriczy attribute it to Bernardino Licino and Loeser to Cavazzola. The attribution to Giorgione was first proposed by Morelli, and followed—with reservations—by Thausing, Berenson, Cook, Justi and Fiocco. As in the case of the Onigo portrait (plate 105), Morassi favors Cariani. Frimmel's attribution to Pordenone appears the most reasonable because of the portrait's resemblance to the Onigo portrait.

Plate 107

GATTAMELATA PORTRAIT. *Canvas, 90 × 73. Florence, Uffizi Gallery.* Cavalcaselle attributes this work to Torbido; Gamba, followed by Borenius, to Cavazzola; Longhi to Giorgione. Gamba confirms now that the Cavazzola attribution appears to be the most acceptable. The metallic colors, the heavy polish, the rather hard, dry modeling discourage identification with the last Giorgione work, especially if one compares this portrait with the *Knight of Malta* (plate 85).

Plate 108

CONCERT. *Canvas, 76 × 99. Hampton Court, Royal Gallery.* Listed as a Giorgione in ancient inventories, this picture is often linked with *The Three Ages of Man* in the Pitti Palace Gallery (plate 109). Morassi sees it as product of Giorgione's school, but L. Venturi noticed a difference of quality which leads one to connect this canvas with the *Master and disciple* formerly in the Cook Collection. Both paintings are far closer to the art of Morto da Feltre. Berenson, however, publishes this picture as "early Giorgione".

Plate 109

THE THREE AGES OF MAN. *Panel, 62 × 77. Florence, Pitti Palace.* Formerly in Prince Ferdinand's Collection, as a product of the Lombard School. This is a puzzling work, with an incredible range of attributions, none of which is entirely convincing. Inghirami and Cavalcaselle believe it to be a Lotto; Morelli, Cook, Suida and, later, Morassi, attributed it to Giorgione; Logan and Gronau attributed it to Morto da Feltre; L. Venturi describes it as "superior to Morto and very Giorgionesque"; Fiocco and, at first, Pallucchini ascribed it to Torbido, but Longhi and, later, Pallucchini thought it by Bellini; Berenson thought it a very late Bellini, but recently published it as "early Giorgione".

The only fact of which we are sure is that this is the work of an unknown Master from the Veneto in the early sixteenth century.

Plate 110

VIRGIN AND CHILD. *Canvas, 44 × 36.5. Leningrad, Hermitage Museum.* Transferred from wood to canvas in 1872. Formerly thought to be by Giambellino's School or by Bissolo, it was first attributed to Giorgione in 1908 by Justi, who changed his mind in 1936. Only Morassi accepted the attribution; Richter is not sure; Fiocco speaks of "Giorgione and restorers". One cannot fail to find a certain Giorgionesque atmosphere in this painting, but, among the many works attributed to the master, this one contains the greatest number of Flemish and Antonello influences. It should be ascribed to an unknown painter from the Veneto of the sixteenth century.

Plates 111–112

SINGER and THE MUSICIAN. *Canvases, respectively 112 × 77 and 101 × 75. Rome, Borghese Gallery.* Described as "Giorgione's two buffoons" by Manilli in his book, *Villa Borghese* (1650) and also in a 1693 inventory. An official document of 1833 mentions Giambellino. According to A. Venturi the painter was Domenico Capriolo; Longhi at first thought it by a member of Mancini's group, later ascribing it verbally to Giorgione. This suggestion was developed by Paola della Pergola who explicitly attributed the paintings to Giorgione, with the support of Luciana Ferrara, in 1954. A referendum was then held in which Fiocco insisted on Capriolo; Grassi, Wittgens, Longhi and Zeri voted for Giorgione; Gnudi, though generous in his praise of the quality of the two works, kept his own council. The author finds it difficult to reconcile these paintings with what must reasonably have been Giorgione's last style. Once Titian has been excluded, one should think rather of a provincial follower of Giorgione, who intensified the Master's vibrations and amplified his forms. Perhaps Savoldo, possibly Pordenone, but especially Dosso.

Plate 113

SHEPHERD WITH FLUTE. *Canvas, 52 × 98. Naples, Pinacoteca Nazionale.* Attributed by Berenson to Cariani and by Morassi to Sebastiano del Piombo. The author has reached the same conclusion here as in the case of the two previous works, though this canvas may not be by Dosso.

Plate 114

JUDGEMENT OF SOLOMON. *Canvas, 208 × 318, unfinished. Kingston Lacy (U.K.). Bankes Collection.* Attributed by Wickhoff to Stefano Cernotto, of the Bonifazio Veronese School; by Roger Fry to Catena; by Hourticq to Titian; by Suida, partly, to Sebastiano del Piombo and partly to Giorgione; by Fiocco entirely to Giorgione. Rightly, first L. Venturi, then Longhi, Pallucchini and Morassi attributed the canvas entirely to Sebastiano.

Plate 115

SACRED CONVERSATION. *Panel, 50 × 81. Venice, Gallerie dell' Accademia.* Formerly attributed to Cariani, then to Previtali, later still to a follower of Giambellino. Gronau and L. Venturi associated it with the *Allendale Nativity*, believed at the time to be by Catena, but now Venturi accepts the *Allendale Nativity* as a Giorgione. For Berenson the artist was Previtali; Longhi, followed by Morassi, suggested Giorgione; Pallucchini is decidedly in favor of Sebastiano del Piombo and Fiocco shares his view with reservations; for Dussler too, the painter is Sebastiano. Though admittedly there are some points of contact with the Louvre's *Sacred Conversation*—certainly by Sebastiano—and with the Glasgow

Adulteress—probably by Sebastiano —the last attribution cannot be free of all doubt. Richter's suggestion of Palma should not be too lightly discarded.

Plate 116

SUSANNAH AND DANIEL (also known as *Christ and the Adulteress*). *Canvas, 137 × 180. Glasgow, Corporation Galleries.* This could be identified with the *Adulteress* described as "for sale and a work by Giorgione" in a letter by Camillo Sordi to Francesco Gonzaga Duke of Mantua of 1612. A copy by Cariani is in Bergamo's Accademia Carrara. The Glasgow painting had been attributed to Cariani by Cavalcaselle; to Domenico Campagnola by J. P. Richter; to Sebastiano, then to Titian, then to Giorgione by Berenson; to Romanino by A. Venturi and Gombosi; to Giorgione by Bode, Cook, Morelli, Justi and Hermanin; by L. Venturi, Pallucchini and generally the other moderns to Titian. Richter believes the canvas was begun by Giorgione and finished by Titian. In the author's view Sebastiano is more plausible.

Plate 117

CONCERT. *Canvas, 108 × 122. Florence, Pitti Palace.* Bought as a Giorgione in 1654 by Cardinal Leopoldo de' Medici, this painting could be the same one recalled by Ridolfi in the Florentine Collection of Paolo del Sera: attributed by Morelli to Titian, by Wickhoff and Hadeln to Domenico Campagnola, by Hourticq to Sebastiano del Piombo. Gronau believed it to have been begun by Giorgione and finished by Titian; in the opinion of many modern critics (Suida, Tietze, Morassi), it was painted entirely by

Titian. The old attribution to Giorgione is still accepted by Cook, Richter, Fiocco and now also by L. Venturi. The intense drama of the scene, however, the thin color paste, and especially the feverish eyes of the monk suggest very strongly the hand of Titian. Compare this canvas with Titian's Ancona *Madonna* and with the *Portrait* in the Lansdowne Collection.

Plate 118

PORTRAIT OF A MAN. *Canvas, 75 × 62·5. Washington, National Gallery of Art, Kress Collection.* Attributed to Giorgione by Cook, Borroughs, Morassi (with reservations), and, rightly so, to Titian by Berenson and L. Venturi. D. Phillips notes that "the facial expression, intense with the suggestion of inward conflict, and the structural simplification of the forms are eloquent of Giorgione".

Plate 119

ST GEORGE. *Panel, 124 × 65. Venice, Cini Collection.* Attributed to Giorgione by Waagen; Berenson calls it a fragment and claims that the Saint's head is modern. Borenius, Fiocco, Gronau, consider it a Palma, and Longhi believes it a Titian, painted about 1511. This appears the most acceptable attribution, but perhaps Titian painted it a few years later.

Plate 120

STORM AT SEA. *Canvas, 305 × 405. Venice, Gallerie dell'Accademia.* Recalled as by Giorgione by Vasari in the first edition of the *Lives*, and as by Palma in the second edition. This work, in extremely poor condition, is partly by Palma and partly by Paris Bordone.

Other works have been attributed to Giorgione, but with so little justification that they do not merit reproduction in this book. They are: *Portrait of a Della Rovere* (Vienna, Kunsthistorisches Museum: possibly by Pellegrino da San Daniele); *Portrait of Ariosto* (?) (London, National Gallery: Titian); *Portrait of a Grimani* (?) (New York, Metropolitan Museum: Titian); *Portrait of a Musician* (Rome, Palazzo Venezia: Titian); *Man in Fur Coat* (Munich Gallery: Palma); *The Bravo* (Vienna, Kunsthistoriches Museum: Palma); *Young Faun* (Munich Gallery: Palma); *Orpheus and Eurydice* (Bergamo, Accademia Carrara: Palma); *Apollo and Daphne* (Venice, Seminario; Palma); *Birth of Adonis* and *The Forest of Polydorus* (Padua, Museo Civico: both by Romanino); *Dead Christ* (Treviso, Monte di Pieta': Francesco Vecellio); *Portrait* (Paris, Gentilli Collection: perhaps by Pordenone); *Young Man* (Brunswick, Herzog Anton Ulrich Museum: School of Palma); *Portrait* (New York, Bache Collection: School of Palma); *Portrait* (Rome, Borghese Gallery: School of Pordenone).

WORKS MENTIONED BY SOURCES AND DOCUMENTS OF THE XVI AND XVII CENTURIES

INSCRIPTIONS:

1. June 5, 1506; *Laura* (plate 41).
2. 1508: *Portrait* (plate 90).

DOCUMENTS:

3. 1507: A *Telero* for the Audience Hall of the Doge's Palace (lost).
4. 1508: Frescos on the façade of the Fondaco dei Tedeschi (plates 94 and 95).

TADDEO ALBANO, letter of November 7, 1510:

5. *Night* (Creche), in the home of Taddeo Contarini (identified by some as the painting in plate 100a).
6. *Night* (Creche), in the home of Vincenzo Beccaro (identified by some as the painting on plate 33).

MARCANTONIO MICHIEL, *information about works of art:*

In the home of Taddeo Contarini, 1525:

7. "The canvas, in oils, of the three philosophers in a landscape, two standing and one sitting down, and contemplating the rays of the sun, with that stone so admirably painted, was begun by Zorzo of Castelfranco and finished by Sebastian the Venetian" (plate 48).
8. "The great oil canvas showing Aeneas and Anchises in Hades . . .", (identified by some with the painting in plate 21).
9. "The canvas of a landscape with the birth of Paris, and two shepherds standing by, was painted by Zorzo of Castelfranco and was one of his first works" (identified by some as the picture in plate 23; see also plate 96b).

In the home of Gerolamo Marcello, 1525:

10. "The portrait of the very same M. Hieronimo in arms, showing his back down to the waist, and turning his head" (lost).
11. "The canvas with the nude Venus, sleeping in a landscape, with a little Cupid by her side, was painted by Zorzo of Castelfranco, but the landscape and the Cupid were finished by Titian" (generally identified as the picture in plate 68).
12. "Half-length figure of Mr Hieronimo, reading" (lost).

In the home of Giannantonio Venier, 1528:

13. "Half-length figure of a soldier, armed but not wearing his helmet" (lost).

In the home of Gabriele Vendramin, 1530:

14. "The small canvas of a landscape, with a storm, a gypsy woman, and a soldier" (plate 54).
15. "The dead Christ upon his tomb, supported by an angel, was painted by Zorzo of Castelfranco and reconditioned by Titian" (mistakenly identified by some with the *Dead Christ* of Treviso).

In the home of Giovanni Ram, 1531:

16. "The head of a young shepherd with fruit in his hand" (lost).

17. "Head of a youth with an arrow in his hand" (generally identified as the picture in plate 63).

In the home of Antonio Pasqualino, January 5, 1532:

18. "The head of a lad holding an arrow in his hand was painted by Zorzo of Castelfranco, and Pasqualino has received it from Giovanni Ram, though Ram still possesses a copy of it, which he believes to be an original" (see above, n. 17).

19. "The head of St James with a pilgrim's staff was painted by Zorzo of Castelfranco, or copied by one of his pupils from the Christ in the Church of San Rocco." (The copy has been lost; the original is shown in plate 83.)

In the home of Andrea Oddoni, 1532:

20. "The nude St Jerome sitting in the desert in the moonlight was copied from a canvas by Zorzo of Castelfranco" (lost).

In the home of Michele Contarini, August 1543:

21. "The ink on paper nude in a landscape was drawn by Zorzo" (lost).

In the home of Marcantonio Michiel, August 1543:

22. ". . . This is the nude by Zorzo himself, which is in my possession" (lost).

In the home of Pietro Bembo, in Padua, undated:

23. "The two small paintings on goatskin, in vermilion, are by Giulio Campagnola; one is a nude woman copied from Zorzo, reclining and turned" (lost).

In the home of Pietro Servio, note added 1575:

24. "A portrait of his father by Zorzo of Castelfranco" (lost).

PAOLO PINO, *Dialogue on painting,* 1548:

25. "St George, whose figure is reflected in the water and, on the sides, by two mirrors" (lost).

LUDOVICO DOLCE, *Dialogue on Painting,* 1557:

26. "Frescos on the Fondaco dei Tedeschi" (see above, n. 4).

PARIS BORDONE, *evaluation in the Giovanni Grimani Home, 1563:*

27. "A crèche" (identified by some as the picture in plate 33).

VASARI, *Lives,* Second Edition, 1568:

In the home of the Patriarch of Aquileia, Grimani:

28. "A head for a David (said to be his own portrait), with hair coming down to the shoulders" (plate 62).

29. "A larger head of a man, holding in his hand the red beret of a Commander" (lost).

30. "The head of a cherub or boy, with hair like goatskin" (lost).

In the Borgherini home in Florence:

31. "The portrait of Giovanni as a young man and in the same picture the portrait of the master who was his teacher . . ." (lost).

In the home of Anton de' Nobili:

32. "The head of an armed captain, said to be one of the Captains which Consalvo Ferrante took with him to Venice" (lost).

In Consalvo Ferrante's home:

33. "The great Consalvo himself, armed" (lost).

Shown at the Fair on Ascension Day (1566?):

34. "Portrait of Leonardo Loredano . . . when he was Doge" (lost).

At Faenza, in the home of Giovanni (Bernardi) from Castelbolognese:

35. Portrait of Giovanni Bernardi's father-in-law (lost).

In the Soranzo home at San Polo:

36. Frescos on the façade with "many pictures and stories and other fanciful paintings of his . . . an oil painting on plaster . . . and a spring" (lost).

Fondaco dei Tedeschi

37. Frescos on the façade (see above, n. 4).

Church of San Rocco:

38. "Christ carrying the Cross, and a Jew pulling at Him" (see above n. 19).

Locality unknown:

39. "He painted a nude figure with its back turned to the spectator. At the feet of the figure a limpid stream reflected the front, while a mirror on one side and a burnished corselet on the other reflected the profiles. By this beautiful fancy Giorgione wished to prove that painting is the superior art, requiring more talent and greater effort." (See under Paolo Pino, n. 25.)

In the home of Giovanni Cornaro:

40. Portrait of Caterina Cornaro (lost).

In the home of Giorgio Vasari, from the "Book of drawings":

41. "A head painted in oils, copied from a German of the Fucheri family" (lost).

CARLO RIDOLFI, *The marvels of art,* 1648:

In the Parish Church of Castelfranco:

42. "The panel of Our Lady with Our Lord the Child . . . on the left side St George, in which he portrayed himself, and on the right side St Francis" (plate 42).

In Giorgione's home at San Silvestro:

43. On the façade "oval frescos, with musicians, painters and other fancies inside, and upon the chimneys groups of children . . . in chiaroscuro. . . . Two half-length figures it appears represent the Emperor Friedrich I and Antonia da Bergamo who, having gripped a dagger, is about to kill herself to protect her virginity" (lost).

In the Soranzo home at San Polo:

44. Frescos upon the façade: "stories, friezes, of child and figures in niches, . . . the figure of a woman with flowers in her hand, and in another the figure of Vulcan who is whipping Eros" (see above, n. 36).

In Paolo del Sera's home:

45. "Three portraits . . . upon the same canvas" (plate 117).

In the home of Grimani ai Servi:

46. Frescos on the façade with "nude women" (lost).

In Campo Santo Stefano:

47. Frescos of half-length figures upon a façade (lost).

House overlooking the Canal at Santa Maria Zobenigo:

48. Frescos on the façade "ovals with half-length figures of Bacchus, Venus or Mars . . . grotesques in chiaroscuro . . . and children" (lost).

In the Cassinelli home in Genoa:

49. "Allegories of human life and half-figures: 'nurse with child, armed warrior', a 'young man disputing with philosophers, among merchants and an old woman', 'an antique nude'" (lost).

In the home of Andrea Vendramin:

50. "Self-portrait as David holding Goliath's head, between a knight and a soldier" (lost).

FONDACO DEI TEDESCHI:

51. Frescos upon the façade (see above, n. 4).

In the Marcello home:

52. "A nude sleeping Venus, with Cupid at her feet and a small bird in her hand . . . finished by Titian" (see above, n. 11).

In the home of G. Battista Sanuto:

53. "Bust of woman in gypsy clothing" with her right hand on a book (lost).

In the Leoni home at San Lorenzo:

54. David giving the head of Goliath to Saul (lost).
55. Judgement of Paris (lost: there are many copies of it. See plates 97a and b).

In the Grimani home at San Marcuola:

56. Judgement of Solomon "with the Rabbi's figure unfinished" (identified by some as the picture in plate 114).

In the home of Cavalier Gussoni:

57. Madonna with St Jerome and other figures (lost).

In the home of Senator Domenico Ruzzini:

58. Portrait of a "Captain in armor" (lost).

In the Contarini home at San Samuele:

59. Portrait of a "Knight in black armor" (lost).

In the Malipiero home:

60. Half figure of St Jerome reading a book (lost).

In the home of Niccolo' Crasso:

61. Portrait of the philosopher Luigi Crasso (lost).

In the Annunciata Church at Cremona:

62. St Sebastian (lost).

In the home of Prince Aldobrandini in Rome:

63. Three-quarter length figure of St Sebastian (lost).

In the home of Prince Borghese in Rome:

64. David (lost).

In the home of the Muselli Family in Verona:

65. Young man in fur coat (lost).

In the home of the Van Voert family in Antwerp:

66. Self-portrait as David with the head of Goliath (see above n. 28).
67. Portrait of a "Commander" General (see above n. 29).
68. Portrait of a youth in armor, in which his hand is reflected (lost).
69. Portrait of a German of the Fulchera family, with a fox fur-coat, "seen from the side and turning about". (Probably the "Man in fur coat" attributed to Titian, now in Munich. See above, n. 41).
70. Half length of a nude "in green cloth" (lost).

In the Doge's Palace at Venice, Great Council Hall:

71. Episode of the Emperor Friedrich kissing the foot of Pope Alexander III (lost).

At Venice, unspecified locality:

72. "Celius Plotius attacked by Claudius", half figures. (This is the so-called *Bravo*, by Palma, now in Vienna.)

73. "Portrait of an ancient King" (lost).

Unspecified localities:

74. Portrait of Doge Agostino Barbarigo (lost).

75. Portrait of Caterina Cornaro (see above, n. 40).

76. Portrait of the Great Consalvo (see above, n. 33).

77. Portrait of Doge Leonardo Loredano (see above, n. 34).

78. The doctoring of cats (lost).

79. Nude woman and shepherd with pipe (lost).

80. Twelve pictures portraying the story of Psyche (lost).

81. The ascent to Mount Calvary with Veronica (lost).

82. Large head of Poliphemus wearing a hat (lost).

83. "Cassones" with "fables from Ovid's Golden Age: Jupiter smiting the Giants; Deucalion and Pyrrha; the serpent Python killed by Apollo; Apollo and Daphne Io, Argus and Mercury; the death of Phaethon; Diana and Callisto; Mercury and Apollon's flocks; the rape of Europa; Cadmus in Thebes; Diana and Actaeon; Venus, Mars and Vulcan; the killing of Niobe's sons; Baucis and Philemon; Theseus and Ariadne; Alcides, Deianira and Nessus; the love story of Apollo and Hyacinth; the love story of Venus and Adonis." Some of these were "reduced to small panels" and made up of "many studies". (Probably the whole long description is just a literary essay on the part of Ridolfi, aimed at impressing his erudite contemporaries, with no concrete reference to particular works, with the exception of the following.)

In the home of the Vidmani family:

84. Cassone with stories of Adonis: "his birth, . . . his sweet embraces with Venus . . . his killing by a boar. . . ." (lost).

DAVID TENIERS, *Theatrum pictorium*, 1669:

In the collection of Archduke Leopold Wilhelm in Brussels:

85. "The birth of Paris" (see above, n. 9).

86. "The Ambush" (lost).

LOCATION OF PAINTINGS

AMSTERDAM

LANZ COLLECTION

Allegory of Chastity (plate 20).

BERLIN

KAISER FRIEDRICH MUSEUM

Portrait of a youth (plates 66, 67).
Ceres (plate 100b; attribution).

BOSTON

GARDNER MUSEUM

Christ carrying the Cross (plate 82).

BRUNSWICK

HERZOG ANTON ULRICH
MUSEUM

Self-portrait (plate 62).

BUDAPEST

MUSEUM OF FINE ARTS

The Finding of Paris (plate 23;
fragment).
Portrait of Antonio Broccardo (plate
106; attribution).

CASTELFRANCO
VENETO

CHURCH OF SAN LIBERALE

*Madonna with SS Francis and
Liberale* (plates 42, 43, 44, 45, 46).

CASA PELLIZZARI

Frescos (plates 2, 3, 4, 5, 6, 7, 8, 9,
10).

CASA ROSTIROLLA

Fresco (plate 1).

CHIAVARI

LANFRANCHI COLLECTION

Judgement of Paris (plate 97b; copy).

DRESDEN

GEMÄLDEGALERIE

Sleeping Venus (plates 68, 69, 70,
71).
The Horoscope (plate 96a; copy).
Judgement of Paris (plate 97a; copy).

FLORENCE

UFFIZI

Judgement of Solomon (plates 12, 14).
Trial of Moses (plates 13, 15).
Knight of Malta (plate 85).
Gattamelata Portrait (plate 107;
attribution).

PITTI PALACE

The Three Ages of Man (plate 109;
attribution).
Concert (plate 117; attribution).

LOESER COLLECTION

The Finding of Paris (plate 96b;
copy).

FRANKFURT

STAEDEL INSTITUTE

The Finding of Romulus and Remus
(plate 101; attribution).

GLASGOW

CORPORATION GALLERIES

Susannah and Daniel (plate 116;
attribution).

HAMPTON COURT

ROYAL GALLERY

Bust of Shepherd with Pipe (plate 65).
Concert (plate 108; attribution).

KINGSTON LACY (U.K.)

BANKES COLLECTION

Judgement of Solomon (plate 114; attribution).

LENINGRAD

HERMITAGE

Judith (plates 38, 39).
Virgin and Child (plate 110; attribution).

LONDON

NATIONAL GALLERY

Adoration of the Magi (plates 25, 26, 27, 28, 29).
Man in Armor (plate 47).
Homage to a Poet (plate 99; attribution).
Four Stories of Thyrsis and Damon (plates 102, 103; attribution).

PRIVATE COLLECTION

Aeneas and Anchises (plate 21).

MADRID

PRADO

Madonna with SS Anthony of Padua and Roch (plates 80, 81).

MAIDSTONE

ALLINGTON CASTLE, CONWAY COLLECTION

Story of Paris (plate 104; attribution).

MILAN

PINACOTECA AMBROSIANA

Page (plate 98; copy).

RASINI COLLECTION

Judith (plate 11).

NAPLES

PINACOTECA NAZIONALE

Shepherd with flute (plate 113; attribution).

NEW YORK

FRICK COLLECTION

Portrait of a youth (plate 88).

DUVEEN BROTHERS COLLECTION

Portrait of a lady (plate 40).

NORTHAMPTON

CASTLE ASHBY, NORTHAMPTON COLLECTION

Country Landscape (plate 22b).

OXFORD

ASHMOLEAN MUSEUM

Madonna reading (plate 24 and color plate I).

PADUA

MUSEO CIVICO

Leda and the Swan (plate 16).
Pastoral Scene (plate 17).

PARIS

LOUVRE

"Concert Champêtre" (plates 72–73, 74, 75, 76, 77, 78, 79).

ÉCOLE DES BEAUX-ARTS

The Viola Player (plate 93a; drawing).
Head of an old man (plate 93b; drawing).

PRINCETON (New Jersey)

UNIVERSITY MUSEUM
Paris on Mount Ida (plate 22a).

RICHMOND

COOK COLLECTION
Portrait of Giovanni Onigo (plate 105; attribution).

ROME

PALAZZO VENEZIA
Double portrait (plate 89).

BORGHESE GALLERY
Singer (plate 111; attribution).
The Musician (plate 112); attribution.

ROTTERDAM

BOYMANS MUSEUM
View of Castelfranco (plate 92; drawing).

SAN DIEGO

FINE ARTS SOCIETY
Portrait of a man (plates 90, 91).

VENICE

ACCADEMIA
Gypsy and Soldier (plates 54, 55, 56, 57, 58, 59, 60 and color plate III).
Portrait of an old woman (plate 61 and color plate IV).
Fragment of a nude (plate 94a).
Sacred Conversation (plate 115; attribution).
Storm at Sea (plate 120; attribution).

CHURCH OF SAN ROCCO
Christ with Cross and other figures (plates 83, 84).

SPANIO COLLECTION
Warrior with Page (plates 86, 87).

CINI COLLECTION
St George (plate 119; attribution).

VIENNA

KUNSTHISTORISCHES MUSEUM
Portrait of Laura (plate 41).
The Three Philosophers (plates 48, 49, 50, 51, 52, 53 and color plate II).
Youth holding arrow (plate 63).
David with head of Goliath (plate 64)
Nativity (plate 100a; attribution).

WASHINGTON

NATIONAL GALLERY OF ART
Landscape with Nymph and Cupid (plate 19).
Holy Family (plates 30, 31, 32).
Allendale Nativity (plates 33, 34, 35, 36, 37).
Portrait of a man (plate 118; attribution).

PHILLIPS COLLECTION
Allegory of Time (plate 18).

SELECTED CRITICISM

I will shut the mouths of those who would defend sculpture, as did Giorgione da Castel Franco, our celebrated artist as good and worthy of honor as any of the ancient masters. He confounded for ever the sculptors by painting a picture of an armed St George standing with his feet near the edge of a limpid stream, into which all his figure was reflected; then he painted a mirror, set up against a tree trunk, which reflected the whole of the Saint's back and one side; he added another mirror opposite, which revealed the other side of St George, and thus he proved that a painter can show an entire figure at one glance, which a sculptor cannot do. This work of his was perfectly seen and understood as combining the three parts of painting, which are design, invention, and color.

PAOLO PINO,
Dialogo di Pittura, 1548.

Now Giovanni Bellini and the other masters of that time were not accustomed to study the antique, but copied what they saw before them, and that in a dry, hard, labored manner, and this Titian also acquired.

But in or about 1507 Giorgione da Castelfranco, not liking this method, began to paint in a very beautiful manner. He did not neglect to work from life, or to use natural color, and he painted directly in color without a drawing. He held that this was the best way, shading with colder or warmer tints as the living object might demand. But in doing this he did not perceive that it is impossible to arrange a composition intelligibly without first sketching the forms and grouping them in different ways, for the fancy needs actually to see the design, in order to form a correct judgement.

GIORGIO VASARI,
*The Lives of the most eminent Architects, Painters and Sculptors
of Italy from Cimabue to our days*, First edition, 1550.

Then there was an artist greatly thought of, but of whom much more could have been expected, of whom we have seen some oil paintings so lively, and so fluid around the contours, that no shadows can be perceived. He died, this valiant man, of the plague, and his death was a great loss to art.

LODOVICO DOLCE,
L'Aretino, or *Dialogue on Painting*, 1557.

Giorgione had seen some works by Leonardo, in which the contours were made fluid, and tinged with dark in tremendous measure. This manner he liked so much that as long as he lived he constantly followed it, and imitated it considerably in his oils. As he enjoyed the pleasure of his creations, he strove continuously to put into his work the most beautiful and varied ideas that came to him. Nature had endowed him with such a benign spirit that both in oils and in his frescos he portrayed some very lively things, while other pictures were soft, and harmonic, and fluid in the dark areas, so that many who at the time were considered excellent artists admitted that Giorgione had been born to infuse spirit in his figures, and to reproduce the freshness of a live complexion better than anyone else, not only in Venice, but everywhere.

GIORGIO VASARI,
Lives, Second edition, 1568.

While Florence was acquiring fame thanks to Leonardo, so the name of Venice, thanks to the excellence of Giorgione da Castelfranco was ringing throughout the world. He was educated in Venice and applied himself so intensely to art that he surpassed in painting Giovanni and Gentile Bellini, and gave such life to his figures, that they looked alive. RAFFAELLO BORGHINI,
Il Riposo, 1584.

Giorgione da Castelfranco was greatly fortunate in depicting fish under the limpid waters, and trees and fruits, and all that he chose, in a beautiful manner.

GIAN PAOLO LOMAZZO,
Treatise on the art of painting, 1584.

(Poem in Venetian dialect, free translation):

> Zorzon, you were the first, it is well known,
> To fashion marvels with your paints and brushes;
> And as long as the world and Men shall last
> Your greatness shall never be forgotten.
>
> Until you appeared, all other artists had
> Created statues, whilst you made live figures
> And with the magic of your colors you
> Have given them a truly human soul.

MARCO BOSCHINI,
The Chart of Pictorial Navigation, 1660.

In painting he discovered a softness of touch with the brushes that had never existed before him, and one must confess that his strokes are so much flesh and blood; but his manner, on the other hand, is so rich and easy that one cannot speak of pictorial fiction, but rather of natural reality, because in the softness of his contours, in the placing of lights and "mezze tinte", in the reds, in the strengthening or lowering of his hues, he created such a pleasing and faithful harmony that one should describe his art as painted Nature, or naturalized painting. The ideas of this artist are all solemn, majestic or important, corresponding as they do to his name of Giorgione, and that is why his genius was seen to be directed towards grave figures, with heavy berets upon their heads, with bizarreries of plumage, old-fashioned clothing, shirts that are visible under their tunics, and blown out sleeves with slits in them, breeches in the style of Giambellino but of a more beautiful shape; his materials are silk, velvet, damask, wide stripes of satin; other figures wear armors as polished as mirrors; his was the real Idea of human actions.

MARCO BOSCHINI,
The rich minefields of Venetian painting, 1664.

It is known to everyone that Giorgio, or Giorgione da Castel-franco, was one of the first of us to release painting from the narrowness of its previous conditions. It was he who gave to it the genuine character of art. By allowing his genius to wander freely he departed from the beaten track of simple reasoning, which can control only science, and added to solid knowledge the capricious flights of fancy in order to attract and to please. The very moment he had mastered the excellent principles, he began to feel the greatness of his genius, being as it was full of fire, and of a certain natural violence; thus he emerged flying from his old timidity and infused a life which had previously been lacking in the painted figure, however well organized this may have been by his masters. In his hands colors achieved an accomplished taste, and he succeeded in portraying to perfection the cool reality of real flesh. He gave a new rotundity and vigor to painted objects, and thanks to the liveliness of his spirit he achieved a veracity never seen before. Aptly, he flashed lights upon shadows, which always appear rather sharp in reality, and most of all handled his dark masses with complete freedom, at times cleverly increasing their intensity beyond the natural one, at other times, making them more tender and serene by giving them unity and softness of contour, so that the parts included between those masses could be seen and yet not seen. This method, to everybody's eyes, increased the greatness of the artist's style, though only few could understand the reason for it.

ANTON MARIA ZANETTI,
On Venetian Painting and Public works of the Venetian masters, 1771.

From the days of his apprenticeship in the Bellinis' workshop, and being guided by a spirit which knew its own strength, he disdained that pettishness which still prevailed, and replaced it with that freedom of action, almost with that contempt, which is the quintessence of art. In this he was an inventor, that no one before him had known that manner of handling the brush, so resolute and strong, so capable of surprising the eye, especially when it came to distances.

He then went on to make his manner greater, by broadening his contours, renovating his perspectives, giving life to the ideas reflected in the faces and gestures, carefully selecting his draperies and accessories, softening his passages from one color to another, and finally by strengthening and giving much greater effect to his "chiaroscuro".

LUIGI LANZI,
History of Italian painting, 1796.

Giorgione was certainly a great artist, indeed one of the greatest that the Renaissance ever produced. On the other hand one cannot deny that there is a greatness which he could never achieve: the field of ascetic idealism never appealed to him. . . . But apart from this he was the inspirer of a revolution involving every branch of art, and which gave an exclusive character to the products of his vigorous brush.

ALEXIS-FRANCOIS RIO,
On Christian Art, 1836.

There could be reason for assuming that Giorgione was the first of Venetian moderns to follow in Bellini's footsteps and in attaching importance to the landscape. If we accept the tradition still alive in our days no one was his equal, at the end of the fifteenth century, in composing country scenes; no one could achieve the pure elegance of the figures which animated these landscapes. The landscapes familiar to Giorgione do not have the rocky character or the towering heights found by Titian in the Cadore region. No Dolomites project their sharp summits against the pure skyline; there are, instead, elms and cypresses, vines and mulberry-trees, hazel-bushes and poplars, graceful undulations, woods, farm-steads and battlements; and in all this there is variety, without repetitions.

CROWE AND CAVALCASELLE,
History of Painting in Northern Italy, 1871.

By no school of painters have the necessary limitations of the art of painting been so unerringly though instinctively apprehended, and the essence of what is pictorial in a picture so justly conceived, as by the school of Venice. . . . At last, with final mastery of all the technical secrets of his art, and with somewhat more than "a spark of the divine fire" to his share, comes Giorgione. He is the inventor of "genre", of those easily movable pictures which serve neither for uses of devotion, nor of allegorical or historic teaching . . . morsels of actual life, conversation or music or play, but refined upon or idealized, till they come to seem like glimpses of life from afar. . . . He is typical of that aspiration of all the arts towards music, which I have endeavored to explain—towards the perfect indentification of matter and form.

WALTER PATER,
The School of Giorgione, 1877.

Giorgione did not display all his powers until the six last years of his short life, approximately from 1504 to 1511. In the few of his works which have come down to us . . . his original and eminently poetical intelligence shines so purely, his simple and honest artistic temperament speaks to us so strongly and attractively, that whomsoever has heard him once shall never forget him. No other painter can, as he, enrapture our fantasy with such an economy of means, and captivate our spirit for hours upon end; and yet, at times, we do not even know what his pictures mean.

IVAN LERMOLIEFF (G. MORELLI),
The Works of Italian Masters, 1880.

Giorgione's life was short, and very few of his works—not a score in all—have escaped destruction. But these suffice to give us a glimpse into that brief moment when the Renaissance found its most genuine expression in painting. Its overboisterous passions had quieted down into a sincere appreciation of beauty and of human relations. It would be really hard to say more about Giorgione than this, that his pictures are the perfect reflex of the Renaissance at its height.

BERNARD BERENSON,
The Venetian Painters of the Renaissance, 1894.

71

The problem of opened or closed contours was for Giorgione a motive of uncertainty. He had been trained by his master Giovanni Bellini to feel the beauty of a contour, even to prefer the refined beauty of a line. The magnificent oval of the Dresden Venus is still conceived as a closed contour, even though the delicate touch of its *sfumato* gives it a dreamlike quality. But when Giorgione added the soldier's figure to *Gypsy and Soldier*, he had no need for definite outlines, and in fact that image is typically a pictorial one, an open form, sketched out. . . .

This form of his which emerged from closed contours found its natural basis in the zones of color. And color was for Giorgione a conception of his fantasy even before becoming a feeling.

LIONELLO VENTURI,
Giorgione and Giorgionism, 1913.

The uncertainty of his craftsmanship is a further proof of how little Giorgione owed to the Venetian school. Even in the *Castelfranco Madonna*—the three figures of which, in spite of everything, are derived from Bellini's iconographic material— the faces and draperies belong to someone who, out of ignorance or contempt, would rather lose himself in his own innovations than follow the beaten road. A face, a wrinkle, a hand are difficulties that each and every craftsman has been taught to overcome; but surely it is not here that Giorgione proved himself a master. Apart from some problems to which he was able to find the solution—a rock, foliage, and especially some feminine faces—Giorgione will go down as a technician more curious than impeccable. And his weaknesses confer upon him a reputation for independence which certainly does not diminish him in the eyes of the moderns. Two particular reasons appear to justify his fame as an open innovator: his landscapes and his nudes, and also the combination of landscape and nude. Of all his landscapes the most beautiful is obviously the vision, so right and so new, of the Castelfranco walls growing pale under a thunderstorm. The man who was able to see and to portray such an effect is surely one of the painter-poets who have added to the poetry of nature the beauty of painting.

LOUIS HOURTICQ,
The Problem of Giorgione, 1930.

Some of his admirable creations appeared in the houses of the most exclusive lovers of art: intimately religious subjects; mythological, idyllic, fanciful themes—or at times hermetical compositions of a philosophical and literary nature—suddenly enriched the Venetian repertoire, pouring new blood into its trite iconography. A new spirit was being expressed in a lyrical, dream-like atmosphere, but this new spirit was also to the highest degree observant of nature in its most attractive and emotional aspects. A new taste for color was finding its way, vibrating with intensity of stress, and at the same time softened by an exquisite blending of tonalities.

This was a new light, enveloping everything in intangible gold-dust, and obtained by a technique so very different from the much vaunted Flemish method: this technique consisted in superimposing flashes of bright color to the chromatic structures beneath, or conversely in diminishing their brightness into an ashen-like blending of hues: this paved the way to Vecellio; these were the foundations of modern art.

ANTONIO MORASSI,
Giorgione, 1942.

Giorgione can only be understood in the light of Antonello da Messina. His great victory was in fact the addition of the Venetian chromatic taste to the Sicilian master's revelation; Giorgione brought into power Antonello's reform which, being free from the Flemish realistic minutia, was no longer compelled to "breathe big", and could finally adapt itself to a subtler, more idealistic and more human world, penetrating each fiber of it and exalting it with the power of color, finally aware of its constructive function.

73

His subtle passages from the generic to the specific, granting the same dignity to the landscape and figures, and respecting each person's individuality, for each one is a world; that movement of his picture inside the air, which came directly from his soul; that dramatic enveloping of each object with live atmosphere, was never fully appreciated, busy as people were with the dialectics of attribution.

So that, whereas a few undisputed and undisputable works would have sufficed—perhaps just the two pillars of the *Castelfranco Madonna* and of the *Gypsy and Soldier*—to prove that Giorgione was both renovated and a renovator, the student of this master has to proceed among the shifting sands of the various theories and sympathies, where it is easy to become bogged down, and not difficult to sink for ever.

GIUSEPPE FIOCCO,
Giorgione, 1942.

Giorgione's art is certainly a complex one in its developments, in its aesthetical interests and in its cultural values, so much so that from its origins it caused many different interpretations of its figures, many contradictions and numerous reactions in the field of historiography. Giorgione's taste is not as exclusive as Tintoretto's or Carpaccio's: from the nucleus of his inspiration —strictly connected with color and light, and therefore to tonality—an ever changing jet of invention spurts forth, possibly taking different directions. Giorgione's cultural thirst, based upon his interest in the currents of his time, had the gift, common to all geniuses, of expressing itself on every occasion, through a purely fantastic and lyrical process, in a perfect work of art. The practical result of this sensitivity of his, for ever active, was that in the field of invention all the links with the iconographic tradition of the fifteenth century, both religious and profane, were broken. With Giorgione a new representational mythology was born, in which man was put in touch with nature, to the extent where nature itself at times chose to become a protagonist;

a new dignity enriched the characters' psychology and they, in their isolation, became introspective. . . . His revolution in the artistic field consisted not only in a transformation of his subjects, but in a total renewal of representational sensitivity.

RODOLFO PALLUCCHINI,
Venetian Painting of the 16th Century, 1944.

His timidity was still present when he painted the Castelfranco Altarpiece, a composition which, far from being a revolutionary discovery, did not more than replace the old and sublime perspective formula of Bellini with the one, elegantly decorative —between ogival and pyramidal—so familiar to the traditions of Umbria and Emilia in the last decades of the fifteenth century, with what advantage I would not dare to say. . . .

These first cautious experiments of Giorgione the "pre-Raphaelite" lasted till he painted the *Gypsy and Soldier*. This work also is rather bound and, here and there, difficult to read, nor is it entirely free from the Emilian influences but . . . as a whole it indicates a return to the traditional chromatic principles of Venice, and an approaching change, perhaps even a reversal, of the master's previous experiences.

This reversal was perfectly understood, biographically speaking, by Vasari who, when writing about Giorgione at the beginning of his *Life of Titian*, made a completely different statement from the previous one. Had he forgotten that he had already described Giorgione as a follower of Leonardo's *sfumato*? He had not forgotten, but now he was referring to the second and last Giorgione, the Giorgione of the "modern manner", even though such a manner was exactly the opposite of that of Raphael and Michelangelo.

ROBERTO LONGHI,
Five centuries of Venetian Painting, 1946.

That intimate concentration of each single figure, that suspension of all movement, that silence, are all expressions of Giorgione's feeling as opposed to Titian's. This exuberant artist (Titian) reveals from his very first works a search for movement, for eloquence of gesture, peasant models, overladen draperies, tricks of light due perhaps to a passing cloud or two, crowded compositions. But here (in Giorgione's works), all is calm, spiritual concentration, sense of space, harmony of rich and intense colors.

CARLO GAMBA,
"My Giorgione", in *Arte Veneta*, 1954.

BIBLIOGRAPHICAL NOTE

The main source of information about Giorgione's works is the so called *Anonimo Morelliano*, by M. A. Michiel, the correct title of which is *Notizie d'opere sul disegno*; this was written between 1525 and 1543, and published by J. Morelli in 1800. For further biographical information about the artist the reader is advised to refer to the exemplary *Giorgione* by Antonio Morassi Milan, 1942), the bibliography for which goes as far as 1939. The author lists below only the milestones in critical literature on Giorgione, with the addition of the most recent works.

B. CASTIGLIONE. *Il Cortegiano*, Venice 1524.
P. PINO. *Dialogo di pittura*, Venice 1548.
G. VASARI. *Le Vite*, Florence 1550; second edition, Florence 1568.
L. DOLCE. *Dialogo della pittura*, Venice 1557.
R. BORGHINI. *Il riposo*, Florence 1584.
G. P. LOMAZZO. *Trattato dell'arte della pittura*, etc., Milan 1584.
C. RIDOLFI. *Le maraviglie dell'arte*, Venice 1648.
M. BOSCHINI. *La carta del navegar pitoresco*, Venice 1660.
M. BOSCHINI. *Le ricche minere della pittura veneziana*, Venice 1664.
J. VON SANDRART. *Academia nobilissimae artis pictoriae*, Nuremberg 1675.
A. M. ZANETTI. *Varie pitture a fresco de' principali Maestri veneziani*, Venice 1760.
A. M. ZANETTI. *Della pittura veneziana*, etc., Venice 1771.
L. LANZI. *Storia pittorica dell'Italia*, Bassano 1795–6.
J. A. CROWE and G. B. CAVALCASELLE. *A History of Painting in North Italy*, London 1871.
W. PATER. *The School of Giorgione*, London 1877.
I. LERMOLIEFF (G. MORELLI). *Die Werke italienischer Meister*, etc., Leipzig 1880.
A. CONTI. *Giorgione*, Florence 1894.
B. BERENSON. *The Venetian Painters of the Renaissance*, New York 1894.
C. VON FABRICZY. "Giorgione de Castelfranco", in *Repertorium für Kunstwissenschaft* 1896.
H. COOK. *Giorgione*, London 1900.
U. MONNERET DE VILLARD. *Giorgione da Castelfranco*, Bergamo 1904.
L. JUSTI. *Giorgione*, Berlin 1908.
G. GRONAU. "Kritische Studien zu Giorgione", in *Repertorium für Kunstwissenschaft* 1908.
L. VENTURI. *Giorgione e il Giorgionismo*, Milan 1913.
A. VENTURI. *Storia del'Arte Italiana*, IX, 3, Milan 1928.
L. HOURTICQ. *Le problème de Giorgione*, Paris 1930.
J. WILDE. Roentgenaufnahmen der "Drie Philosophen", etc., in *Oesterreiches Jahrbuch N. F.* 1932.

A. FERRIGUTO. *Attraverso i misteri di Giorgione*, Castelfranco 1933.

G. M. RICHTER. *Giorgio da Castelfranco, called Giorgione*, Chicago 1937.

L. COLETTI. "La crisi manieristica nella pittura veneziana", in *Convivium* 1941.

G. FIOCCO. *Giorgione*, Bergamo 1942.

A. MORASSI. *Giorgione*, Milan 1942.

G. DE BATZ. *Giorgione and his Circle*, Baltimore 1942.

R. PALLUCCHINI. *La pittura veneziana del Cinquecento*, I, Novara 1944.

V. MARIANI. *Giorgione*, Rome 1945.

R. LONGHI. *Viatico per cinque secoli di pittura veneziana*, Florence 1946.

L. COLETTI. "La crisi giorgionesca", in *Le Tre Venezie* 1947.

R. WISCHNITZER-BERNSTEIN. "The *Three Philosphers* by Giorgione", in *Gazette des Beaux-Arts*, 1945.

H. TIETZE. "La mostra di Giorgione e la sua cerchia a Baltimore", in *Arte Veneta* 1947.

G. GLÜCK. *Der Weg zum Bild*, Vienna 1948.

H. D. GRONAU. "Pitture veneziane in Inghilterra", in *Arte Veneta* 1949.

K. T. PARKER. *The Tallard "Madonna" in the Ashmolean Museum*, London 1949.

R. PALLUCCHINI. "Un nuovo Giorgione a Oxford", in *Arte Veneta* 1949.

H. TIETZE and E. TIETZE-CONRAT. The *Allendale Nativity*, etc., in *Art Bulletin* 1949.

R. L. DOUGLAS. "Some early Works of Giorgione", in *Art Quarterly* 1950.

R. MARINI. *Giorgione*, Trieste 1950.

F. M. GODFREY. "The Birth of Venetian Genre and Giorgione", in *The Connoisseur* 1951.

A. MORASSI. "The Ashmolean *Reading Madonna* and Giorgione's Chronology", in *Burlington Magazine* 1951.

G. CREIGTON. "On Subject and Non-Subject in Italian Renaissance Pictures", in *Art Bulletin* 1952.

P. DELLA PERGOLA. "Due nuovi Giorgioni", in *Paragone* 1953.

L. COLETTI. *La pittura veneta del Quattrocento*, Novara 1953.

G. FIOCCO, L. GRASSI, R. LONGHI, F. WITTGENS. Answering a referendum, in *La Scuola* 1954.

L. VENTURI. *Giorgione*, Rome 1954.

B. BERENSON. "Notes on Giorgione", in *Arte Veneta* 1954.

W. SUIDA. "Spigolature giorgionesche", in *Art Veneta* 1954.

P. HENDY. "More about Giorgione's *Daniel and Susannah* at Glasgow", in *Arte Veneta* 1954.

C. GAMBA. "Il mio Giorgione", in *Arte Veneta* 1954.

A. MORASSI. "Esordi di Tiziano", in *Arte Veneta* 1954.

M. VALSECCHI. *La Pittura veneziana*, Milan, 1954.

L. COLETTI. "Un tema giorgionesco", in *Emporium* 1955.

REPRODUCTIONS

SOL A VIRTVS
CLARA
ÆTERNA
QVE HABETVR

VMBRA
TRANSITVS
EST
TEMPVS NOSTRVM

Plate 2. FRESCOS, Castelfranco, Casa Pellizzari

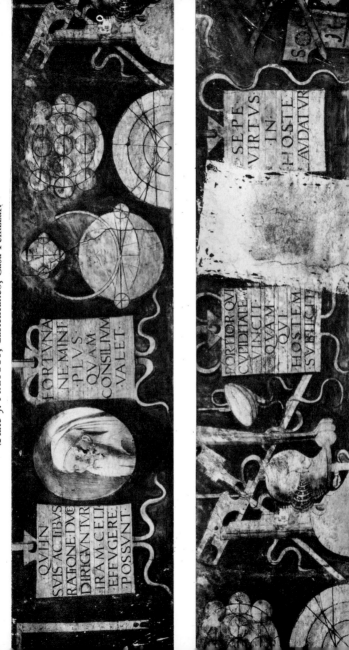

Plate 3. FRESCOS, Castelfranco, Casa Pellizzari

QVI IN
SVIS ACTIBVS
RATIONE DVCE
DIRIGVNTVR
IRAM CELI
EFFVGERE
POSSVNT

FORTVNA
NE MINVS
PLVS
QVAM
CONSILIVM
VALET

SEPE
VIRTVS
IN
HOSTE
LAVDATVR

FORTIOR QVI
CVPIDITATE
VINCIT
QVAM
QVI
HOSTEM
SVBIICIT

SI
PRVDENS
ESSE
CVPIS
IN FVTVRA
PROSPICIAM
INTENDE

Plate 4. FRESCOS, Castelfranco, Casa Pellizzari

Plate 5. FRESCOS, Castelfranco, Casa Pellizzari

Plate 6. FRESCOS, Castelfranco, Casa Pellizzari

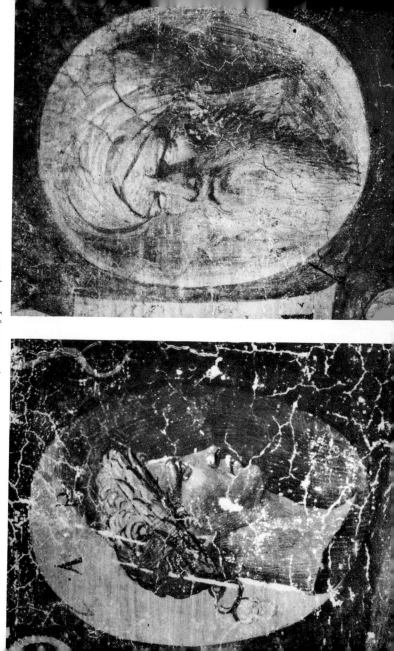

Plate 7. *Details of plates 4 and 2*

Plate 8. *Details of plates 2 and 3*

Plate 9. *Details of plates 3 and 5*

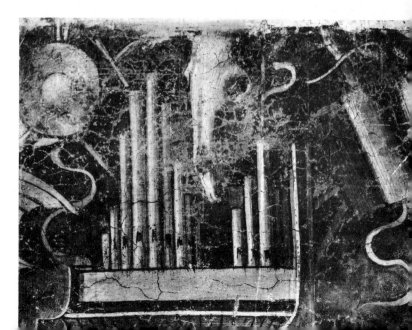

Plate 10. *Detail of plate 4*

Plate 11. JUDITH, Milan, Rasini Collection

Plate 12. JUDGEMENT OF SOLOMON, Florence, Uffizi

Plate 13. TRIAL OF MOSES, Florence, Uffizi

Plate 14. *Detail of plate 12*

Plate 15. *Detail of plate 13*

Plate 16. LEDA AND THE SWAN, Padua, Museo Civico

Plate 17. PASTORAL SCENE, Padua, Museo Civico

Plate 18. ALLEGORY OF TIME, Washington, Phillips Collection

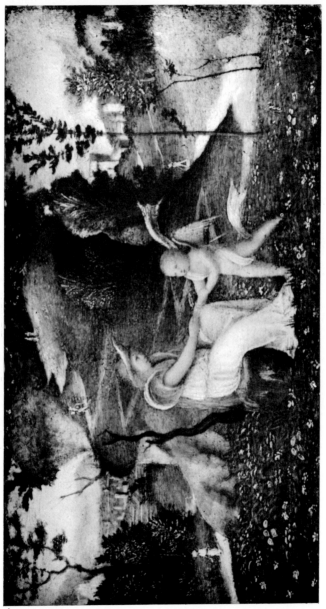

Plate 19. LANDSCAPE WITH NYMPH AND CUPID,
Washington, National Gallery of Art

Plate 20. ALLEGORY OF CHASTITY, Amsterdam, Lanz Collection

Plate 21. AENEAS AND ANCHISES, London, Private Collection

Plate 22. PARIS ON MOUNT IDA,
Princeton, University Museum,
and COUNTRY LANDSCAPE,
Northampton, Castle Ashby

Plate 23. THE FINDING OF PARIS, Budapest, Fine Arts Museum

Plate 24. MADONNA READING,
Oxford, Ashmolean Museum (*detail of color plate* I)

Plate 25. ADORATION OF THE MAGI, London, National Gallery

Plate 26. *Detail of plate 25*

Plate 27. *Detail of plate 25*

Plate 28. *Detail of plate 25*

Plate 29. *Detail of plate 25*

Plate 30. HOLY FAMILY, Washington, National Gallery of Art

Plate 31. *Detail of plate 30*

Plate 32. *Detail of plate 30*

MADONNA READING, Oxford, Ashmolean Museum

Plate 33. ALLENDALE NATIVITY,
Washington, National Gallery of Art

Plate 34. *Detail of plate 33*

Plate 35. *Detail of plate 33*

Plate 36. *Detail of plate 33*

Plate 37. *Detail of plate 33*

Plate 38. JUDITH, Leningrad, Hermitage

Plate 39. *Detail of plate 38*

Plate 40. PORTRAIT OF A LADY,
New York, Duveen Brothers Collection

Plate 41. PORTRAIT OF LAURA,
Vienna, Kunsthistorisches Museum

Plate 42. MADONNA WITH SS FRANCIS AND LIBERALE,
Castelfranco, Church of San Liberale

Plate 43. *Detail of plate 42*

Plate 44. *Detail of plate 42*

Plate 45. *Detail of plate 42*

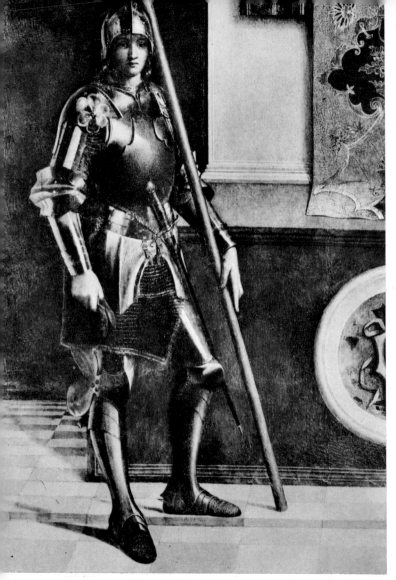

Plate 46. *Detail of plate 42*

Plate 47. MAN IN ARMOR, London, National Gallery

Plate 48. THE THREE PHILOSOPHERS,
Vienna, Kunsthistorisches Museum

THE THREE PHILOSOPHERS, Vienna, Kunsthistorisches Museum
(*detail of plate 48*)

Plate 49. *Detail of plate 48*

Plate 50. *Detail of plate 48*

Plate 51. *Detail of plate 48*

Plate 52. *Detail of plate 48*

Plate 53. *Detail of plate 48*

Plate 54. GYPSY AND SOLDIER, Venice, Accademia

Plate 55. *Detail of plate 54*

Plate 56. *Detail of plate 54*

GYPSY AND SOLDIER, Venice, Accademia (*detail of plate 54*)

Plate 58. *Detail of plate 54*

GYPSY AND SOLDIER, Venice, Accademia (*detail of plate 54*)

Plate 57. *X-ray of part of plate 54*

Plate 58. *Detail of plate 54*

Plate 59. *Detail of plate 54*

Plate 60. *Detail of plate 54*

Plate 61. PORTRAIT OF AN OLD WOMAN,
Venice, Accademia (*detail of color plate IV*)

Plate 62. SELF-PORTRAIT,
Brunswick, H. Anton Ulrich Museum

Plate 63. YOUTH HOLDING ARROW,
Vienna, Kunsthistorisches Museum

Plate 64. DAVID WITH HEAD OF GOLIATH,
Vienna, Kunsthistorisches Museum

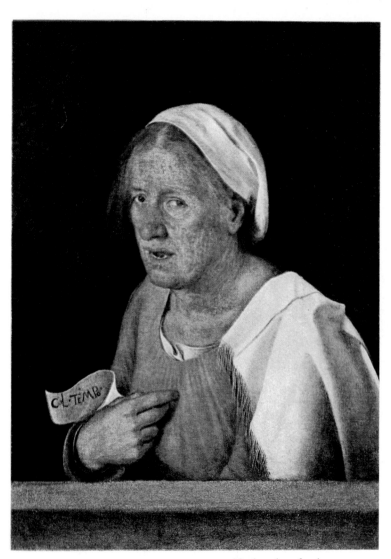

PORTRAIT OF AN OLD WOMAN, Venice, Accademia

Plate 65. PORTRAIT OF SHEPHERD WITH PIPE,
Hampton Court, Royal Gallery

Plate 66. PORTRAIT OF A YOUTH,
Berlin, Kaiser Friedrich Museum

Plate 67. *Detail of plate 66*

Plate 68. SLEEPING VENUS, Dresden, Gemäldegalerie

Plate 69. *Detail of plate 68*

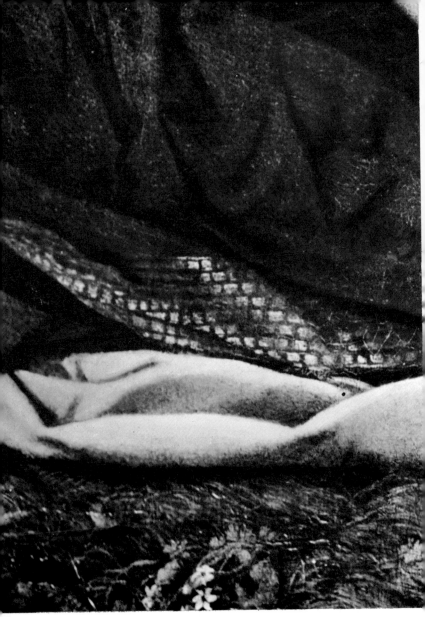

Plate 70. *Detail of plate 68*

Plate 71. *Detail of plate 68*

Plate 72–73. "CONCERT CHAMPÊTRE", Paris, Louvre

Plate 74. *Detail of plates 72–73*

Plate 75. *Detail of plates 72–73*

Plate 76. *Detail of plates 72–73*

Plate 77. *Detail of plates 72–73*

Plate 78. *Detail of plates 72–73*

Plate 79. *Detail of plates 72–73*

Plate 80. MADONNA WITH SS ANTHONY OF PADUA AND ROCH, Madrid, Prado

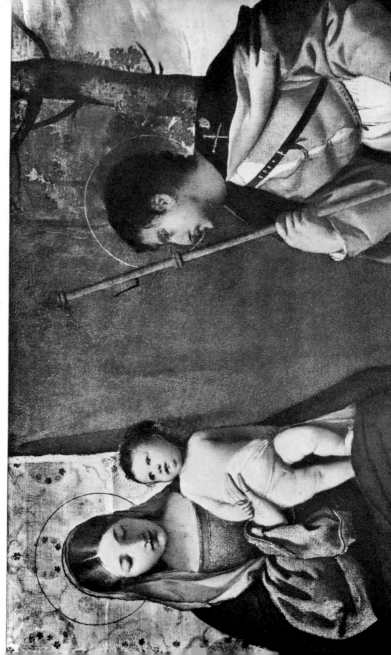

Plate 81. *Detail of plate 80*

Plate 82. CHRIST CARRYING THE CROSS,
Boston, Gardner Museum

Plate 83. CHRIST WITH CROSS AND OTHER FIGURES,
Venice, Church of San Rocco

Plate 84. *Detail of plate 83*

Plate 85. KNIGHT OF MALTA, Florence, Uffizi

Plate 86. WARRIOR WITH PAGE, Venice, Spanio Collection

Plate 87. *Detail of plate 86*

Plate 88. PORTRAIT OF A YOUTH,
New York, Frick Collection

Plate 89. DOUBLE PORTRAIT,
Rome, Palazzo Venezia

Plate 90. PORTRAIT OF A MAN,
San Diego, Fine Arts Society

Plate 91. *Detail of plate 90*

Plate 92. VIEW OF CASTELFRANCO, Rotterdam, Boymans Museum (drawing)

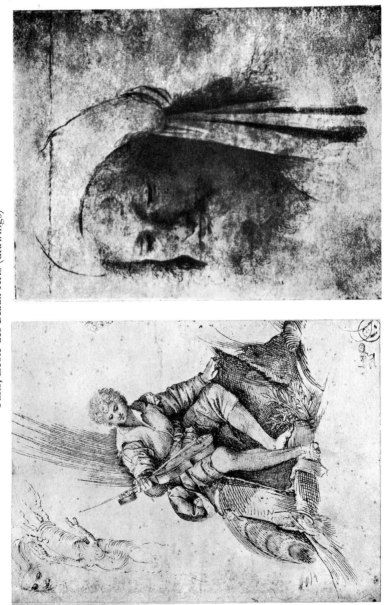

Plate 93. THE VIOLA PLAYER *and* HEAD OF AN OLD MAN,
Paris, École des Beaux-Arts (drawings)

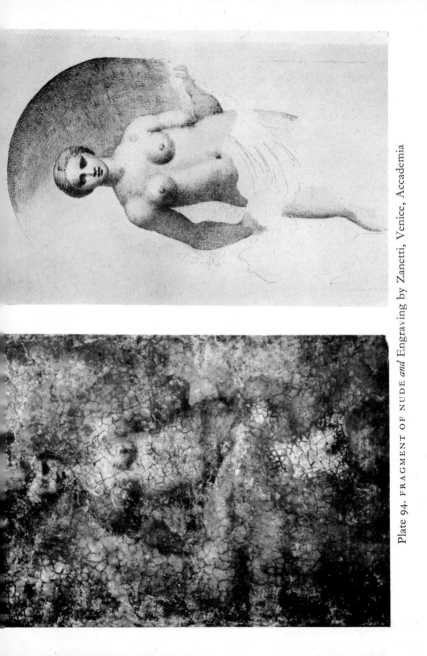

Plate 94. FRAGMENT OF NUDE *and* Engraving by Zanetti, Venice, Accademia

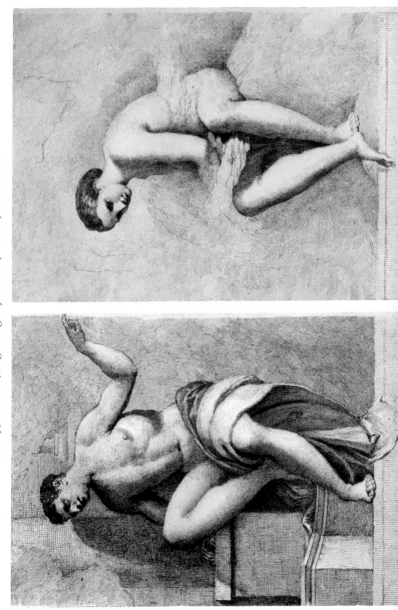

Plate 95. NUDES, engravings by Zanetti, Venice, Accademia

Plate 96. THE HOROSCOPE, Dresden, Gemäldegalerie
and THE FINDING OF PARIS, Florence, Loeser Collection (*copies*)

Plate 97. JUDGEMENT OF PARIS,
Dresden, Gemäldegalerie and Chiavari,
Lanfranchi Collection (*copies*)

Plate 98. PAGE, Milan,
Pinacoteca Ambrosiana (*copy*)

Plate 99. HOMAGE TO A POET,
London, National Gallery (*attrib.*)

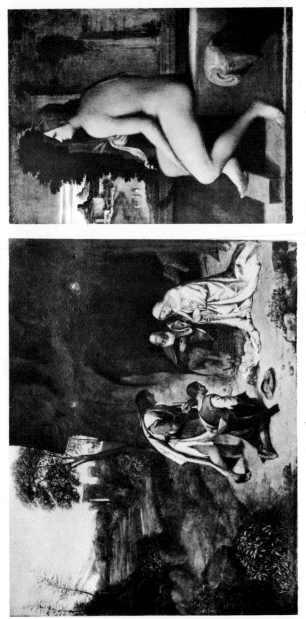

Plate 100. NATIVITY, Vienna, Kunsthistorisches Museum, *and* CERES, Berlin, Kaiser Friedrich Museum (*attrib.*)

Plate 101. THE FINDING OF ROMULUS AND REMUS, Frankfurt, Staedel Institute (*attrib.*)

Plate 102. STORIES OF THYRSIS AND DAMON,
London, National Gallery (*attrib.*)

Plate 103. STORIES OF THYRSIS AND DAMON,
London, National Gallery (*attrib.*)

Plate 104. STORY OF PARIS,
Maidstone, Conway Collection (*attrib.*)

Plate 105. PORTRAIT OF GIOVANNI ONIGO
Richmond, Cook Collection (*attrib.*)

Plate 106. PORTRAIT OF ANTONIO BROCCARDO,
Budapest, Fine Arts Museum (*attrib.*)

Plate 107. GATTAMELATA PORTRAIT,
Florence, Uffizi (*attrib.*)

Plate 108. CONCERT, Hampton Court, Royal Gallery (*attrib.*)

Plate 109. THE THREE AGES OF MAN, Florence, Pitti Palace (*attrib.*)

Plate 110. VIRGIN AND CHILD,
Leningrad, Hermitage (*attrib.*)

Plate III. SINGER, Rome, Borghese Gallery (*attrib.*)

Plate 112. THE MUSICIAN,
Rome, Borghese Gallery (*attrib.*)

Plate 113, SHEPHERD WITH FLUTE,
Naples, Pinacoteca Nazionale (*attrib*.)

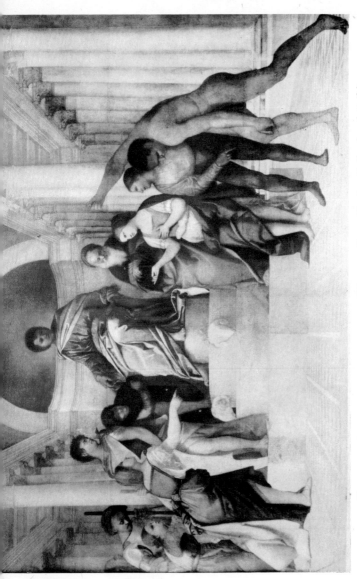

Plate 114, JUDGEMENT OF SOLOMON, Kingston Lacy, Bankes Collection (*attrib.*)

Plate 115. SACRED CONVERSATION, Venice, Accademia (*attrib.*)

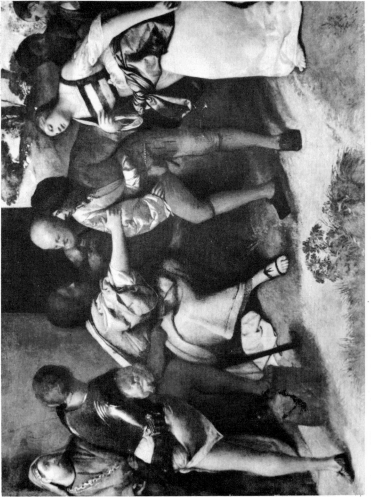

Plate 116. SUSANNAH AND DANIEL, Glasgow, Corporation Galleries (*attrib.*)

Plate 117. CONCERT, Florence, Pitti Palace (*attrib.*)

Plate 118. PORTRAIT OF A MAN,
Washington, National Gallery of Art (*attrib.*)

Plate 119. ST GEORGE, Venice, Cini Collection (*attrib.*)

Plate 120. STORM AT SEA,
Venice, Accademia (*attrib.*)